The Teacher's Guide to Understanding and Supporting Children with Literacy Difficulties In The Classroom

from the author

Understanding and Supporting Children with Literacy Difficulties
An Evidence-Based Guide for Practitioners
Dr Valerie Muter
Foreword by Professor Margaret Snowling
ISBN 978 1 78775 057 9
eISBN 978 1 78775 058 6

The Parent's Guide to Understanding and Supporting
Your Child with Literacy Difficulties
Dr Valerie Muter
ISBN 978 1 83997 706 0
eISBN 978 1 83997 707 7

My Special Alphabet Book
A Green-Themed Story and Workbook for Developing Speech Sound
Awareness for Children aged 3+ at Risk of Dyslexia or Language Difficulties
Valerie Muter and Helen Likierman
Illustrated by Jane Dorner
ISBN 978 1 78775 779 0
eISBN 978 1 78775 780 6

of related interest

The British Dyslexia Association – Teaching Dyslexic Students
Theory and Practice
Edited by Lynn Lowell
Foreword by Dr Helen Ross
ISBN 978 1 78775 745 5
eISBN 978 1 78775 746 2

Assessment for Dyslexia and Learning Differences
A Concise Guide for Teachers and Parents
Gavin Reid and Jennie Guise
ISBN 978 1 78592 522 1
eISBN 978 1 78450 911 8

THE TEACHER'S GUIDE TO

Understanding and Supporting Children with Literacy Difficulties
In The Classroom

Dr Valerie Muter

Jessica Kingsley Publishers
London and Philadelphia

First published in Great Britain in 2025 by Jessica Kingsley Publishers
An imprint of John Murray Press

2

A CIP catalogue record for this title is available from
the British Library and the Library of Congress.

ISBN 978 1 83997 704 6
eISBN 978 1 83997 705 3

Printed and bound in the United States by Integrated Books International

Jessica Kingsley Publishers' policy is to use papers that are natural,
renewable and recyclable products and made from wood grown in sus-
tainable forests. The logging and manufacturing processes are expected
to conform to the environmental regulations of the country of origin.

Jessica Kingsley Publishers
Carmelite House
50 Victoria Embankment
London EC4Y 0DZ

www.jkp.com

John Murray Press
Part of Hodder & Stoughton Limited
An Hachette UK Company

Contents

Acknowledgements 7

Introduction 9

Part 1: The Knowledge

1. Beginning to Read: It's About Cracking a Code 23

2. Moving Beyond Cracking the Code 37

3. When Literacy Development Goes Wrong 51

4. Not All Dyslexic Children Look the Same 69

5. Why Many Dyslexic Children Have More Than Literacy
    Difficulties: Co-occurrence. 81

Part 2: How to Support and Help

6. How We Identify and Assess Literacy Difficulties 103

7. Identifying and Assessing Co-occurring Difficulties 131

8. How We Teach Children with Literacy Difficulties 149

9. Supporting the Child with Literacy Difficulties in the
    Classroom 171

10. How to Support the Child with Co-occurring
Difficulties. 193

11. Some Broader Management Issues and What to Do If
Your Pupil Has a Complex Difficulty. 219

Closing Comments. 235

Glossary 237

References 241

Resources 245

Index. 251

Acknowledgements

In 2021, I published a book titled Understanding and Supporting Children with Literacy Difficulties: An evidence-based guide for practitioners. This book drew on my 35 years of clinical and research experience and was aimed at practitioners in the field of literacy difficulties (psychologists, speech and language therapists, specialist literacy teachers and SENCos) who wanted to have a research-based understanding of the nature of literacy difficulties and how this links to practice. More recently I decided that it would be helpful to write two further books that are essentially companion books to the original practitioner guide – one for parents and one for class teachers. In so doing, I would be able to share with a broader readership what I have learned from my clinical and research experiences and would like to pass on. Encouraged by my editor, Amy Lankester-Owen of Jessica Kingsley publishers, this is the second of the two companion books – geared towards helping classroom teachers better understand their pupils' literacy difficulties and what causes them, and even more importantly, guiding them towards how they can support their pupil to become a more confident and secure reader and writer.

I would first like to thank Elizabeth Shaw who read the first full draft of the book and advised me on how I could make the contents most accessible and useful to class teachers. Amy Lankester-Owen provided helpful guidance as I worked through the first chapters and then again at the final editorial stage. I am grateful to David Chamberlain who created a number of figures and diagrams and who provided a lot of morale boosting along the way.

I should like to thank my research and witing collaborators including Professor Margaret Snowling, Professor Charles Hulme and Dr Helen Likierman. And lastly, a special thanks must go the thousands of children I have worked with clinically and who have participated in my research projects without whom I could not have amassed the knowledge that enabled me to write this book.

Introduction

This book is for class teachers who want to know more about literacy difficulties and how they impact classroom learning. The topics I will cover include recognizing and identifying literacy difficulties, setting in place accommodations for these and supporting the child's learning within the classroom context. Given the high prevalence of literacy difficulties (around 8% of our child population, but likely to be currently much higher because of the impact of Covid-19 and home schooling), this book should prove a valuable resource for class teachers concerned about individual children's struggles with literacy.

Why is learning to read so important? Arguably, it is the single most important educational challenge a child faces during their first two to three years of school life. The child who learns to read easily will usually have a positive attitude towards reading that sees them through into adulthood. Also, early readers find learning in the classroom easier; so much of what children learn in class is through reading from the whiteboard or through the books teachers ask them to read. In contrast, children who struggle to learn to read may feel very negatively towards books and can even become resistant readers. In avoiding books, they are at risk of failing at school – which of course later on restricts their further study and job opportunities. Poor readers often become anxious and frustrated, which then affects them psychologically. Because of the many challenges that children with literacy difficulties experience, it is not surprising that there is wide interest among parents and teachers as to how best to support them.

Struggling to learn to read is a common problem. Reception and

Year 1 teachers will be aware that a child in their class is having difficulty if they are observed to:

- be slow to learn the letters of the alphabet
- struggle to remember key words they have seen many times in the books they read
- find it hard to get the hang of phonics.

Quite a few late readers will have difficulties of spoken language too — evident as having a limited vocabulary, not always understanding instructions, finding it hard to put words together to form sentences, and difficulties in pronouncing words correctly. Of course, some children just need a little more time to settle into school routines before they are ready to learn how to read and write — for instance, children with summer birthdays who are young for their class, children for whom English is not their first language and children who may not have had nursery school experience. It is reasonable to give these children a little more time and space to get started. But by the time a child reaches the end of Year 1, they should know all the letters of the alphabet, they should have a 'sight vocabulary' of simple and common words, and they should be able to decode or 'phonically sound out' two-, three- and four-letter words. At this stage, most schools carry out a phonics screener check with their pupils; if a child fails, this will alert most teachers to their reading difficulties, even if they have not been so worried before.

There are of course some children who appear to get off to a reasonable start in learning to read but then struggle later on in primary school; as a teacher, you will have noticed that their speed of reading is slow, they are probably reluctant to pick up a book, and spelling is hard for them. These children will need help in their middle primary years to 'kick start' their progress in reading and spelling and to restore their motivation and confidence.

I have worked as a paediatric cognitive psychologist for over 40 years. This has involved assessing children who have learning difficulties, sometimes in clinic settings like hospitals and sometimes in research studies. Many of these children have what we call

developmental learning disorders. Examples of developmental disorders include:

- dyslexia (reading and spelling difficulties)
- developmental language disorder (speech and language difficulties)
- dyscalculia (arithmetic difficulties)
- attention with hyperactivity disorder (attention/ concentration difficulties)
- developmental coordination disorder/dyspraxia (motor difficulties that affect writing skills).

Other children have learning difficulties which are of **neurological** origin; these include children with brain injury, epilepsy, brain tumours and also certain genetic disorders. All in all, I estimate that during my long career in clinical practice and research, I have assessed over 15,000 children! My special interest, both clinically and in my research, has always been literacy difficulties – both dyslexia (which means word-level reading difficulties) and related language difficulties (which affect children's understanding of what they read). Having worked with so many children and their families and teachers, I wanted to share as widely as possible what I have learned from both my research and my clinical practice.

This book aims to help you as a class teacher have a better understanding of what literacy difficulties are; I draw on my own research and on current scientific evidence to explain what causes difficulties in learning to read, write and spell. I then explain how having such a difficulty can impact a child's day-to-day (as well as their school) life. Finally, and most importantly, I provide guidelines, advice and lots of practical tips to enable you to identify the child with a literacy difficulty and to support and reinforce their learning, so that they are able to progress better in their literacy skills. A main feature of the book is a series of fictionalized examples of children who illustrate key issues, through which I describe in practical terms how we should assess and teach children with literacy difficulties. I have drawn on my many years' experience as a practising child psychologist to create cases which are an amalgam of children whom I have personally assessed. The fictionalized children first appear in the early chapters of the book when key concepts and issues are described and you will encounter them again in the later chapters that address assessment, identification and teaching.

My original book, *Understanding and Supporting Children with Literacy Difficulties: An Evidence-Based Guide for Practitioners*, was written for professionals (psychologists, speech and language therapists and specialist teachers) who work with children with literacy difficulties. In this book, I share my knowledge with you as class teachers, bearing in mind that you are very likely to have at least five or six children in your class of say 30 who are experiencing difficulties in learning to read. You may not be involved directly in carrying out formal assessments of children's literacy difficulties or in delivering specialist intervention programmes, but I hope you will come to realize as you work your way through this book that there is much that you can do within the classroom to accommodate for the difficulties these children experience and to support them through the process of learning to read.

The book is split into two parts:

- **The Knowledge:** The first five chapters of the book provide you with a knowledge base drawn from the extensive scientific research that has been carried out in relation to normal and abnormal literacy development. Having this knowledge will enable you to understand what your pupil is experiencing and so put you in the most informed position as to how best to help and support them.
- **How to Support and Help:** The remaining six chapters draw on the knowledge base established in Part 1 to provide evidence-based guidelines that will help you to:
  - first, identify children in your class who have a literacy difficulty
  - second, know how you can support and manage these children so that they have positive learning experiences in the classroom
  - third, select teaching strategies that are most effective so that these children can acquire improved literacy skills.

In this book, you are presented with quite a lot of information. As a busy teacher, you may feel at times rather overwhelmed by the detail, especially if you have only recently embarked on your teaching career and are still building both your knowledge base and your teaching experience. I occasionally describe scientific methods and statistics in research studies which you may find rather daunting, particularly if you don't yourself have a science background. It doesn't matter if you skim through or even skip over the technical details (you can always come back to these when you have more time); it is the findings and conclusions of these studies that you need to be aware of and to take note of. Others among you, who have been teaching for some time, will have already built a much broader knowledge base and have a wealth of teaching experience to draw on. Even so, I hope that you will still find this book useful in extending your knowledge, particularly that which comes from the scientific studies I describe.

To help you target the key features of each chapter, I begin by highlighting the main areas I intend to cover, and at the end of each chapter I summarize the key messages for you to focus on and to take forward. For some of the lengthier sections in a chapter, there are short summary recaps to help you keep track of the main points as you read through the chapter. The body of each chapter provides the in-depth information you can delve into in order to gain more insight. Part 1 (The Knowledge) describes important research studies and their findings. Some readers may want to skim over these details and then move on to focus more of their attention on the practical advice given in Part 2 (How to Support and Help). To help you get to grips with some of the terminology I use when describing research studies and statistics (including assessment statistics), I have created a **glossary** at the end of the book that you can refer to when you come across a term you are unfamiliar with (or have forgotten the meaning of). Also, feel free to dip in and out of and to revisit and re-read sections of the book on an as-needs basis. Some sections are relevant mainly to younger children, others to older age groups – so you might want to dart about to sections that speak to the age and stage of learning your pupil is at.

Part 1: The Knowledge

The first two chapters describe how the typical child learns to read. It is hard to appreciate the underlying issues facing a child with a literacy difficulty unless you have an understanding of the skills that are needed for reading to progress normally.

In **Chapter 1**, I emphasize the **beginning stages of learning to read** in which I show how having a good oral vocabulary, being able to easily learn alphabet letters and knowing how to break up spoken words into sounds together play a huge part in getting the child off to a good start in reading. Scientific research studies and artificial intelligence models have shown us that the first two years of learning to read are essentially about **cracking the alphabetic code** so that children can use their knowledge of sound-to-letter connections (or mappings) to enable them to decode words they've not seen before. Because learning to read is a process that that takes place over a number of years, it is important to take a longitudinal view; this means studying the same child (or children) over several years to see how their reading develops overall – and especially to see what skills and factors are most critical at the different stages of learning to read. I conclude this chapter by grounding what we have covered through making explicit links between specific research findings about early word-level reading development and principles of classroom teaching practice.

In **Chapter 2**, we turn to **later stages in reading development** when oral language skills assume greater importance as children encounter more complex tests. I then go on to look at how environmental factors impact ease of learning to read: we look at whether it is easier to learn to read in some languages than others, how parents reading at home to their children influences their language and early reading development, and of course the crucial role class teachers play in providing quality literacy instruction. Finally, research into the skills children need to develop reading comprehension is described and these facts linked to principles of classroom teaching practice.

In **Chapter 3**, we begin to explore **what literacy difficulties are and what causes them**. You will know from the previous chapters what skills are needed for children to learn to read easily. Could a problem in acquiring some of these key skills be the explanation for literacy difficulties like dyslexia? We look at definitions of dyslexia and how science has shown us that dyslexia is a genetic or inherited difficulty that affects the way the brain is wired. In people with dyslexia, it seems that the left-sided brain regions needed for language processing do not function as they should. This leads to a difficulty at the cognitive (or learning) level, specifically with processing the sounds that make up spoken words. We revisit our artificial intelligence model which points to what might go wrong when its 'hardware' is disrupted. Children with literacy difficulties may appear to be struggling more at some times and less at other times as they grow and develop – which is why we need to take a longitudinal view. I illustrate this by describing Nicholas, a little boy from one of my research studies who was followed from his pre-school days up until the age of ten. Finally, I describe what reading comprehension difficulties are and what causes them.

If dyslexia is caused by a difficulty in processing sounds in words, we should expect dyslexic children to look similar to each other. But in fact, not all dyslexic children look the same – some have mild difficulties, others more severe problems; some have both reading and spelling problems, others just spelling difficulties; some have attention problems, some don't; some have handwriting difficulties, some don't; some are good at maths, others aren't. In **Chapters 4** and **5**, we look at these **individual differences** and what explains them. We also see that many dyslexic children not only have literacy problems but they are very likely to have other difficulties too; these are called **co-occurring difficulties** – and they include weaknesses in maths, attention and motor skills. It is these individual differences, and the observation that many dyslexic children have more than one difficulty, that explain:

- differing degrees of dyslexia – from mild through to severe
- how some children have added 'risks' or deficits (like having spoken language weaknesses as well as reading difficulties)

- some children's ability to draw on their special strengths to compensate for their literacy difficulties
- the presence of other (i.e. co-occurring learning/ educational) difficulties that exist alongside the literacy problems and that complicate the picture.

These sometimes tricky concepts are illustrated in a series of four fictionalized children: Alex, who has early speech and language delay and who then goes on to experience dyslexia and also reading comprehension difficulties; Jyoti, who has dyslexia co-occurring with arithmetic difficulties or dyscalculia; Billy, who has dyslexia and co-occurring attention difficulties; and Freddie, who has dyslexia and co-occurring visual motor difficulties or dyspraxia.

Now we move to Part 2 which is very practical and hands-on. Part 2 is about assessment, identification, intervention and management

Part 2: How to Support and Help

Chapter 6 focuses on how we can **identify the child with a literacy difficulty**, starting with what might be evident even before they start school (lateness in talking, muddling speech sounds, being born into a family of poor readers and spellers). I then look at how we might identify children who have dyslexia even after they have been at school for only a short while. Screening for dyslexia is currently very topical and I look at how that can be done in the classroom, through working alongside and with the school's special educational needs coordinator (SENCo) and specialist teachers. Identifying the child with a literacy difficulty is all very well, but we then need to ensure that extra help is set in place so that the child can make better progress – and that progress needs to be monitored. Children who continue to make slow progress need more detailed assessments of their learning difficulties, and I describe what such an assessment should look like. And, I look at how we identify those children whose difficulties are not so evident during their early schooling but who experience problems later on, most usually with spelling. If a child with more than one language is struggling to learn to read, is that due to their having to juggle two languages or could they have a learning difficulty?

I look at characteristics of these **second language learners** and then see if our available screening tests and assessment measures can be used to see if a child who has more than one language has a learning difficulty or not. Alex will be revisited as an example of identifying and assessing a literacy difficulty in a child who has experienced early speech and language delay.

Chapter 7 begins by addressing the importance of being aware that the majority of children presenting with a literacy problem will have at least one **co-occurring (or accompanying) learning difficulty**. These co-occurring difficulties also need to be identified and assessed so we arrive at a full and complete picture of the child's profile of difficulties (and their strengths too). I revisit Jyoti, Billy and Freddie and show how their assessments shed light on how they learn and what their difficulties are beyond the literacy domain. We conclude by looking at how we assess a child who is a second language learner, using a new case study, Susanna, as an example.

Chapter 8 describes what **teaching techniques have been shown to work best with children with literacy difficulties**. Class teachers need to know about the specialist teaching methods, materials and programmes that science has shown us to be effective in improving the literacy skills of poor readers. Some of these will, of course, be delivered by literacy support specialists and SENCos, but some can be implemented or at least reinforced within the classroom context. Older children with literacy difficulties will need support to develop improved 'higher order' skills, like written narrative and study/organization skills. Tempting alternative (biologically based) interventions such as dietary approaches, reflex therapy, tinted lenses and so on are also (critically) evaluated. Finally, interventions for addressing reading comprehension difficulties are described. Alex is revisited as an example of how we use specialist language and literacy teaching methods. The intervention plan for Susanna, our second language learner, completes this chapter.

The focus of **Chapter 9** is to advise you as a class teacher about **what you can do in the classroom context** to support the learning and progress of a pupil with a literacy difficulty. It provides lots of tips for reinforcing literacy skills. Many children who struggle with reading also lack motivation and confidence; we look at how best to boost these. I strongly emphasize the importance of working with specialist teachers and SENCos who are delivering specific intervention programmes – which you can back up and reinforce in the classroom. Recent research has shown us that teaching assistants are a powerful, effective and economic resource in not just reinforcing children's literacy skills but in delivering prescribed intervention programmes. And I talk about how parents can be used as an additional resource, in particular by you giving them advice as to what they can do at home to encourage their child to read, and how they can develop and support good homework practices.

In **Chapter 10**, I describe **interventions for children who have co-occurring difficulties**, including approaches to addressing attention problems, maths difficulties and visual motor problems. Some of these interventions may be school-based, others provided in clinic contexts. I give lots of examples of what class teachers can do to support the child. Jyoti, Billy and Freddie are revisited to provide examples of interventions and teaching strategies that specifically target their co-occurring difficulties.

Chapter 11 has a dual focus. I look first at **broader management strategies**. Many of these are school-based, for instance setting in place accommodations and supports within the classroom, allowing children extra time in written tests and examinations and the use of technology. And second, I describe how to get help for **children with literacy difficulties who have very complex learning profiles**. These are children who have several learning difficulties and also quite often either health or psychiatric/psychological problems. I then describe the extra help that can be given to such children through the Education, Health and Care (EHC) Plan. As an example of the level of complexity needed for a child to qualify for an EHC Plan, I describe one final case study, Leila, who was born extremely prematurely and has multiple learning and psychological difficulties.

The book also includes some checklists, charts and activities that you may wish to use to support your pupil's literacy progress. These are marked with ★ and can be downloaded from www.jkp.com/catalogue/book/9781839977046.

By the end of this book, I hope that you as a class teacher will have a better understanding of what has caused a pupil's struggles with reading and writing, and how these literacy difficulties impact their learning in the classroom and indeed their day-to-day life in general. Additionally, I hope that you will feel in a more confident position to recognize and identify the child's difficulties and needs, and to know what interventions and support mechanisms you might set in place at school to ensure both their good educational progress and (just as importantly) their psychological well-being.

PART 1

THE KNOWLEDGE

Chapter 1

Beginning to Read:
It's About Cracking a Code

In this chapter I describe how:

→ getting off to a good start in learning to read leads to a lifetime habit of reading
→ phonological awareness (i.e. being able to recognize and analyse sounds in spoken words) plays an important part in helping children begin to learn to read
→ ease of learning the letters of the alphabet is important too
→ children need to be able to make connections (or links) between letters and sounds so that they can acquire the alphabetic principle – which is like cracking a code
→ artificial intelligence models help us understand how children learn to read a new word by forming connections or 'mappings' between sounds and letters that become stronger the more often they see the word.

Reading is the key route to learning about the world around us, whether that is through reading a book or studying a computer screen. It follows that achieving good reading skills is an essential goal for all children. Indeed, reading is the gateway to almost every other subject, and to children discovering their own unique interests and talents.

It is important to realize that learning to read is not the same as, for instance, learning to talk. Most pre-school children acquire spoken language simply by hearing speech at home and in their broader environment, including at nursery. They do not need to be directly taught how to speak. They build up a vocabulary of spoken words and they learn about the structure and rules of spoken language without being aware that they are doing so – as long as they are raised in an environment where they hear speech. In a sense, they learn to talk by instinct. This is not the case for written language; children need to be explicitly taught how to read, write and spell.

Most children have no difficulty learning to read and even at age seven can read a wide range of books. However, there is a sizeable number of children who struggle to learn to read and spell. As many as one in six children fail to read at a level that enables them to make sense of their school curriculum. Not only does failing to learn to read affect a child's educational development; it can also have serious consequences for their emotional well-being and their mental health. Children who learn to read easily develop positive attitudes to reading that can stretch well into adulthood. Anne Cunningham and Keith Stanovich (1997) are researchers who followed a large group of children from age six over the next ten years to see how much reading for pleasure they did and how well they understood and remembered what they read. The children who made a good start in reading at age six were by the age of 16 reading many more books and with a far better understanding and recall of what they read than those who had made a slow start. First, this study shows that making a successful early start in reading clearly has a positive effect on how much we read and enjoy books; and second, the study explodes the myth that children who make a slow start in learning to read 'catch up and are okay in the end'.

As a teacher, you are likely to have several children in your class who struggle with literacy. Some children have problems with all aspects of this important skill – reading accuracy and fluency, spelling and writing skills. Others seem to 'do okay' in reading but find spelling and writing a challenge. In order to understand why these children struggle to acquire literacy skills, it is important to first have an appreciation of the underlying skills that are needed for reading to progress normally. What we know about how children learn to read and why this can sometimes go wrong comes largely from scientific research that takes what we call a **predictor approach**. This involves our identifying either children's learning skills or aspects of their environment that determine or **predict** whether they will be good or poor readers. Generally, we do this by studying two groups of children, children we call **typically** (or normally) developing and children who are at high risk for developing reading problems (these might be children who, for example, are born into families in which several members are known to have literacy difficulties).

We will concentrate in this and the next chapter on typically developing children; this is important for two reasons. First, knowing what skills are important to learning to read helps us develop the best classroom teaching methods that will work for all (or certainly most) children. Second, knowing what skills are needed to learn to read might suggest where the underlying difficulties are in children who struggle to learn to read (which will be the focus of Chapter 3). The most commonly studied predictors of how easily children learn to read are **cognitive** (or learning) skills that research has shown us contribute to literacy development. These skills can be easily defined, they can be measured through giving children simple tests to do, and they can be improved through teaching. However, there are also aspects of the **environment** that are important to literacy development, including the language in which the child is learning to read and parental influences which predict progress in reading – we will look at these in the next chapter.

The first two years at school are really important

The first two years of learning to read are especially important, for two reasons. First, it is during this time that the child 'cracks the alphabetic code', which is the first step to becoming an independent reader. This means that that they come to understand how the printed letters that they see on the page of their book represent speech sounds. Second, there is a lot of evidence to show that reading skills stabilize from about the age of eight onwards; we see very little change in reading patterns after this age. It is not surprising therefore that most research into reading development has concentrated on these important early years.

Cognitive predictors are those specific learning skills and the knowledge base that children need to have in place to enable them to begin to learn to read. These cognitive skills enable us to predict (admittedly with some degree of error) which children will find reading easy and which will find it difficult. The most studied of the cognitive predictors of reading are **phonological skills** – that is, the child's awareness of the sounds they hear in spoken words and their ability to recognize, process and manipulate these sounds. The connection between children's phonological skills and their learning to read is a main focus of this chapter.

Phonological awareness has a powerful influence
What is phonological awareness?
Children's phonological awareness is their understanding of the sound structure of spoken words. It is a skill that develops and becomes more refined as they move from pre-school into the early years of school:

- Children first become aware of hearing and understanding **whole words.**
- They then begin to recognize **syllables**, so 'carpet' is a whole word made up of two syllables – 'car' and 'pet'.
- Even before children start school, they begin to be aware of and to appreciate **rhyme** (i.e. understanding that words like 'pat' and 'sat' rhyme with each other).
- Once they are on the way to learning to read, children are able to recognize phonemes in words. The phoneme is the smallest pronounceable unit of sound in a word; 'p', 'e', 'sh', 'th' are examples of phonemes.

How can we measure phonological awareness?
Phonological awareness can be measured by giving children tasks to do that ask them to identify or analyse sounds in spoken words, some tasks being more difficult than others.

- At the simplest level, children can be asked to identify, segment or blend syllables within words that have two or more syllables; for instance, asking them to tell you the beginning syllable (or 'beat') in the word 'carpet' (answer: 'car'), or asking them to say 'carpet' without the first syllable 'car' (answer: 'pet').
- Children enjoy learning and reciting nursery rhymes as pre-schoolers; after they start school and begin to learn the letters of the alphabet, they are able to identify rhymes (so they can say whether two words they hear rhyme or not) and to produce rhymes (they can think of other words that rhyme with a given word like 'sat' – 'pat, fat, mat' and so on).
- Around the same time, they are able to identify and blend phonemes in words, for example telling you that the first sound in the word 'cat' is 'c', and that the sounds 'c', 'a' and 't' can be joined together to make the word 'cat'.
- A little later on, they are able to segment (for instance, delete or 'take away') beginning and end sounds within words, for example 'cat' without the 'c' says 'at', and 'keep' without the 'p' says 'kee'.
- More advanced phonological skills, like deleting middle sounds from words (e.g. 'stick' without the 't' says 'sick') can be seen in many seven- and eight-year-olds.

How does phonological awareness influence learning to read?
Phonological awareness has a powerful impact on learning to read. This has been demonstrated in research studies that have shown a strong relationship (or correlation) between a child's score on a phonological awareness task (like the ones I describe above) and their score on a reading test (that for instance, asks them to read single words or a story out loud). **Longitudinal studies** have shown us that phonological awareness is also a **predictor** measure of learning to read. In longitudinal research, the same group of children is studied over a period of usually two to three years in order to look at how their literacy skills develop and, most impor-tantly, which early learning measures best predict later progress in learning to read. One of my longitudinal research studies (Muter *et al.*, 2004) has shown that:

- children who have good phonological awareness usually become good readers; in contrast, children who have poor phonological awareness may find it hard to learn to read
- children who have a good oral vocabulary find breaking words into sounds easier than children who have a limited vocabulary; this suggests that phonological awareness and therefore reading too are built on a foundation of oral language
- the best single predictor of a child's reading ability is how easily they learn to identify the individual letters of the alphabet (this is a powerful but temporary effect and is the case only during the first two years at school)
- for children to make the best progress in learning to read, they need to make a meaningful connection between their awareness of sounds in spoken words and their knowledge of the alphabet letters (this is sometimes called **phonological linkage**).

Phonological linkage and the alphabetic principle

When young children make a link or connection between their ability to recognize phonemes in words and their knowledge of the alphabet letters, they have acquired the **alphabetic principle**. Brian Byrne in 1998 defined the alphabetic principle as children's understanding that 'the letters that comprise our printed language stand for the individual sounds that comprise our spoken language' (Byrne, 1998, p.1). This means that children realize that whenever a particular phoneme occurs in a word, and in whatever position, it is represented by the same letter. While this seems both simple and obvious, acquiring the alphabetic principle is a major step for children encountering print for the first time. It is children's understanding of the alphabetic principle that enables them to 'crack the code' that forms the foundation on which all later literacy progress depends. In practical terms, it means that children can now use a phonic decoding or 'sounding out' strategy when they come across printed words they have never seen before. Most children can use this strategy by the time they have completed their first two years at school, and they use this as a building block to broaden and expand their reading vocabularies. It is thus not surprising that reading patterns stabilize thereafter – that is, reading patterns change relatively little from the age of eight onwards.

LET'S RECAP

For children to acquire the alphabetic principle, so important to their early reading development, they must make the link between phonology and print through:

- first, having a minimum level of phonological awareness that enables them to break spoken words into their component sounds
- second, learning the letters of the alphabet
- finally, making a connection between their phonological awareness and their experience of printed words.

Can artificial intelligence tell us how children learn to read?

I've described research studies, including my own, that have pointed to the cognitive skills children need to have in place to enable them to read. Let's now look at this in a rather different way – through **artificial intelligence**, which provides further evidence for learning to read being about making connections or links between sounds and letters. In our technology driven age, we tend to turn a lot to computers to help us understand how the human brain works in relation to developing particular skills – and reading is no exception. We call them **computer simulations** and they are based on the idea that the brain is a large neural network whose function can be replicated by computers. If we can simulate the way humans read by studying how a computer acquires a reading vocabulary, we might come to:

- better understand the processes involved in typical reading development
- arrive at an explanation for how learning to read fails if the neural network (captured by the computer simulation)

is in some way disrupted – as it is presumed to be in children who have a literacy difficulty.

These **connectionist models of reading** are based on complex mathematical calculations, the description of which is well beyond the scope of this book. So, what I will attempt is a brief and simplified explanation of connectionism and how it explains normal reading development. In Chapter 3, we will revisit this to look at how disruption of a component of the reading neural network can offer an explanation of why some children find it hard to learn to read.

The best way to explain complex connectionist models of learning to read is by using a diagram such as the one below (Figure 1.1). The first point to be made within a connectionist model is that when a new word is being learned it is represented in the neural network not as a whole word as such, but instead is distributed across many simple processing elements in what are called **input** and **output** systems.

Let us take the example of the computer learning the new word 'stop':

- The input system encodes the printed letters s, t, o and p, and also their position within the word.
- The output system encodes the phonological features of these letters (i.e. their individual sounds, and the spoken word).

The computer 'trains' the neural network over many trials to learn how to read the word 'stop' by enabling it to develop associations or 'mappings' between the letters (inputs) and their corresponding sounds (outputs).

Our diagram shows the development of the mappings between the sounds and letters of the word 'stop' during training that creates what we call the phonological pathway to reading. Before training has started, there are no connections between the sounds and letters; the computer 'sees' only the letters but cannot come up with the sounds that correspond to these. Over the training trials, the computer performs a set of calculations that generate mappings between the sounds and letters. As training progresses, **partial mappings** emerge between the letters and their corresponding sounds so that by midway through training the word may be partly, though not completely, read correctly – that is, as 'sop' though not 'stop'. By the end of training, **full mappings** between the sounds and letters are in place and the word can then be fully and correctly read as 'stop'.

Before Training:
No mappings evident so word cannot be read

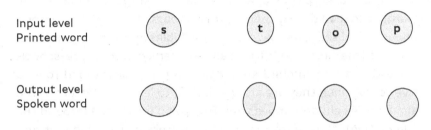

Mid-way Through Training:
Partial mappings emerge so the word may be partly read

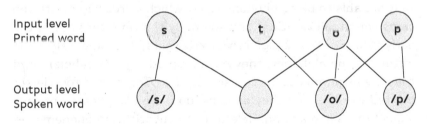

End of Training:
Full mappings are in place so the word is read accurately

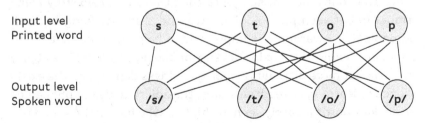

Figure 1.1: Artificial intelligence and learning to read

Bear this model in mind when you come to read Chapter 3 because connectionist models of reading provide a very good explanation of what happens when learning to read goes awry.

How do phonological awareness, letter knowledge and the alphabetic principle work in the classroom?

Let's now consider how children's phonological awareness, letter knowledge and experiences of print relate to their experience of learning to read at school. Figure 1.2 shows the development of the specific phonological awareness skills I have described above in relation to increasing age and also to the stage the child is at in learning to read during their first two years at school. The simpler phonological skills, like segmenting syllables and knowing whether words rhyme, come first. They can be observed in some pre-school-ers and certainly in children in the Reception class (aged four to five years) when they are also beginning to learn the letters of the alphabet. As children move from Reception into Year 1 (around the age of five), they learn more of the letters of the alphabet and begin to build a sight vocabulary of simple and common words. Also, their phonological awareness skills become more refined so they are able to blend phonemes, say which words begin with the same sound (alliteration) and so on. By the time they are in the early stages of Year 2 (aged five to six years), they know all of the letters of the alphabet, they have a broad sight vocabulary and they are beginning to decode simple two-, three- and four-letter printed words – and they can now do more complicated phono-logical tasks like adding, deleting and substituting phonemes in spoken words.

Note that our diagram suggests that there is a **two-way rela-tionship** between phonological awareness and learning to read. Phonological awareness is important to helping children learn to read, but reading also helps develop phonological skills. The ability to carry out more difficult phonological tasks depends on the expe-rience of learning to read; certainly, the ability to delete phonemes in spoken words is rarely seen in children who have not learned the alphabet or developed a sight vocabulary of simple words.

To understand how the model of early reading development I've described in this chapter relates to classroom teaching activities in Reception through to Year 1, see Box 1.1. As a teacher, you will of course be aware that individual schools vary in how they teach phonology, phonics and reading to their early learners. The links I've described between our reading model and principles of classroom teaching assume that the class teacher in this example is adopting a highly structured approach to teaching reading.

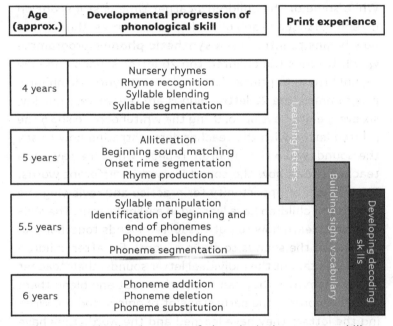

Figure 1.2: The development of phonological awareness skills

Box 1.1: Linking the model of reading development to classroom teaching practice

Term 1 of Reception

In the first term, 'carpet time', is adopted as the teaching framework for developing the children's listening skills, their oral language and their phonological awareness – by 'show and tell' activities, listening to stories, question and answer activities and phonological games of the sort I described earlier. Listening to stories not only helps develop children's listening and oral language skills (including importantly, their vocabulary knowledge); using 'big books' also helps them develop **concepts of print** – essentially what books look like and how they work (that they have a cover page and a title, what print looks like and that it works from left to right, and that words tell a story with a beginning, middle and end).

Terms 2 and 3 of Reception

While some of the children's carpet time is still spent on listening, language and phonological activities, the teacher now begins to introduce a **synthetic phonics** programme which teaches the children the 26 letter sounds and how to 'link' these to printed letters. In most synthetic phonics programmes, the 26 letter sounds are taught very quickly, six every eight days or so, using the whiteboard to show the printed letter, with the teacher demonstrating how to say the sound, while the children 'repeat' what she says. The teacher shows how the sound is used in different words. There is lots of opportunity for practice and reviewing the sounds the children have learned in earlier lessons. The children then learn how to put the letter sounds together (i.e. they blend the sounds to make a word). So, after children have been taught the individual letter sounds, their teacher shows them how they can sound them out and blend them to make words – the early stage of phonic decoding. Writing the letters they have learned and the words they have blended is carried out as an activity at their desks. Common exception words like 'he', 'the' and 'was' are introduced at this stage, teaching them mainly as whole words as they are difficult to sound out and blend. Alphabet books and books that have pictures and which also contain the letters and words the children have been learning are used at school and at home to practise and reinforce letter–sound connections and put children's phonic learning in the context of reading 'real books'.

Year 1

By the start of Year 1, most children have learned all the alphabet letter sounds and know how to blend them to make words and to write simple two- and three-letter words. They are then ready to learn about more complex sounds made up of two letters – 'ay', 'ou', 'ch', 'er' and so on. These are taught in the same way as the single letters, with lots of practice in saying the new sound, hearing it in whole words, blending sounds together to make words, learning how to write the letters that make up the sound and writing them within whole words. Children then move on to spelling the new sound, sometimes orally on the carpet and then writing the spelling as an activity at their desks. More complicated exception words like 'people' and 'because' are taught. Children reading out loud from books (in class and at home) is essential for placing phonics teaching in the context of real-world reading experiences.

By the end of the second year at school, most children experiencing a structured approach to teaching reading, such as that described above, will have developed good early reading skills: they will have a strong sight vocabulary of simple and common words; they can identify and write all the letters of the alphabet and some complex letter sounds; and they can decode and spell simple two-, three- and four-letter words. While individual schools will vary somewhat in how they teach early reading skills, what I have tried to do here is to frame the key features of our reading model (which centres around developing phonological awareness skills, learning letter sounds, building up a sight word vocabulary and beginning to decode words) around what is taught within the classroom – and to place it within the context of the child becoming familiar with books, acquiring oral language skills and realizing how stories work.

KEY MESSAGES TO TAKE AWAY

✓ The first two years of learning to read are about cracking the alphabetic code – children do this by linking their knowledge of sounds in spoken words to their experience of the printed word.

✓ Phonological awareness describes children's awareness of, and their ability to analyse, the speech sound segments of spoken words. Having good phonological awareness is essential for learning to read.

✓ Letter knowledge acquisition is an even stronger determiner of early reading ability, though its role is largely restricted to the first two years of learning to read.

✓ When children combine their phonological awareness with their knowledge of sound-to-letter relationships, they acquire the alphabetic principle – that is, the understanding that the sounds in spoken language are represented by letters in printed language.

✓ Artificial intelligence provides a way of explaining how children acquire the alphabetic principle; computer models show how a new word comes to be read by the forming of connections or 'mappings' between sounds and letters.

✓ It is the acquisition of the alphabetic principle that enables children to phonically decode words they've not seen before; it paves the way to their becoming independent readers.

Chapter 2

Moving Beyond Cracking the Code

Later Stages of Learning to Read, How the Environment Shapes Reading and Reading Comprehension

In this chapter I describe how:

→ processing skills (phonological/auditory memory and naming speed) have an impact on children's reading and spelling
→ children's phonological awareness and processing, measured when they are only five, can predict whether they are likely to be good readers or poor readers at the end of primary school – meaning that these measures might be used in screening for early reading difficulties
→ oral language skills (like understanding grammar and having a wide vocabulary) become increasingly important as children read more complex texts
→ learning to read in English is harder than in other European languages because of its complex spelling structure
→ parents' reading to their children plays an important role in their oral language development and often their reading too
→ children's ability to understand what they read (reading comprehension) depends on the strength of their oral language skills as well as their ability to read words accurately.

The first two years of learning to read are essentially about learning to crack the alphabetic code, that is, learning how to link sounds in spoken words to printed letters. Children can then phonically decode words they have never seen before, which enables them to forge ahead to become independent readers. They don't need their teacher or parent to tell them what a new word says – they can work it out for themselves by 'sounding it out'. Before we look at the later stages of reading development, I want to mention two other phonological skills, beyond phonological awareness, which also play a role, perhaps most importantly after the alphabetic code is cracked – these are **phonological processing** skills.

Phonological processing skills: Memory and naming speed

We have looked in some depth at phonological awareness and its role in the development of reading skills. There are two further skills that exist within the broader phonological domain which also have an influence on literacy, though not quite as strongly or as consistently as phonological awareness; these are **phonological processing** skills.

The first of these phonological processing skills is **phonological memory**, which refers to how we code or represent speech sounds in our short-term memory (it is also sometimes called **auditory working memory**). This takes place in what we call the **phonological loop**. The loop allows for only very brief storage of auditory information (usually sounds or words). However, the storage of auditory information can be lengthened by a **rehearsal** process which refreshes information in the loop. Trying to remember a car registration number you have just been told is an example of storage in the phonological loop; you can remember it for only a matter of seconds but you can retain it for longer through the process of rehearsal – that is, by saying the number over and over again. Having a good phonological/auditory working memory seems to make it easier to learn new words for your vocabulary, whether spoken or written. Although this memory skill is quite strongly related to phonological awareness, it is nonetheless regarded as separate and distinct from it. Examples of phonological memory (or auditory working memory) tasks we might give children include asking them to repeat back:

- a sequence of random spoken digits forwards or backwards, for example say '4-2-1' backwards (answer: '1-2-4')
- increasingly lengthy nonsense words (like 'nolcrid, perplisteronk'); this is a non-word repetition task.

Phonological memory is predictive of reading ability, though its power of prediction is not as strong as either phonological awareness or letter knowledge.

The second phonological processing subskill is **naming speed**. A naming speed task might ask children to name as rapidly as they can sequences of colours, objects, numbers or letters while their speed of doing so is recorded. We think that rapid naming tasks assess the speed and efficiency with which children can retrieve (or 'get at') the sound representations of words in their long-term memory store. Because rapid naming involves scanning across a visual array (of pictures or written letters) while producing a verbal response (naming the picture or letter), it seems to capture what is happening when a child is pronouncing a written word out loud. Naming speed predicts word-level reading ability though not as strongly or as consistently as phonological awareness. Some recent evidence has suggested that there is an especially strong relationship between naming speed and spelling (especially of irregular words) and between naming speed and speed of reading. Children who are good at naming speed tasks seem to spell well and read rapidly while children who are slow to name pictures and letters often misspell irregular words and tend to read slowly.

What happens in the later stages of reading development?
Phonological skills are still needed
Much of the research that we have looked at so far has very much focused on the first two years when children are learning to crack the alphabetic code. What happens after that? Along with my colleague Margaret Snowling (1998), I had the opportunity to follow up a group of 34 children who we had first seen at the ages of five and six years, and who then returned to our study when they were

aged nine to ten years. In this research, we wanted to look at the cognitive skills that are needed later on in primary school when children are having to read more complex texts. First, we found that the children's ability to do a simple phonological awareness task given at ages five to six years (for instance, asking them to delete the beginning or end sound of a word) predicted their ability to do a more complicated phonological task when they were aged nine to ten (for instance, deleting a middle sound from a word). This finding shows us that phonological awareness skills are highly stable over time. If a child is good at doing phonological awareness tasks at age five, they are likely to remain strong in this skill at age ten; conversely, the child who struggles with phonological awareness tasks at age five will likely still find these a challenge even at the end of their primary school years.

Second, we found that the best long-term predictors of reading accuracy skill at age nine to ten were tests of phoneme deletion and non-word repetition that had been given at ages five to six. Finally, we showed that the children's scores on the phoneme deletion and non-word repetition tests given when they were aged five to six predicted with 80 per cent accuracy whether they were described as 'good' or 'poor' readers at age nine to ten. In practical terms, this suggests that giving children simple tests of phonological awareness and processing might form the basis of a screening test that could be used to predict whether children as young as five or six might be 'at risk' for developing literacy difficulties.

And oral language becomes more important later on
Phonological awareness, letter knowledge and the acquisition of the alphabetic principle are essential to children learning how to read at the single-word level. Later on, children have to read increasingly complex texts, which raises the question as to whether broader based language skills begin to play an increasingly important role as children progress beyond single-word reading. In our follow-up study, Margaret Snowling and I found that there was a correlation between the children's ability to read stories accurately at age nine and their understanding of grammar, such as, for instance, their knowledge of word endings like 'ed' endings which indicate past tense (as in 'walked', 'parked' etc.). However, grammar knowledge

did not predict their performance on a single word reading test. As text becomes more complex and content related, grammatical knowledge (and also other language skills like the size of the child's vocabulary) comes to play an increasingly important role. This suggests that children draw on context and content clues in stories (and their knowledge of vocabulary and grammar) to guide the pronunciation of a word that they might not easily recognize if it were on its own — so improving their reading accuracy. For instance, a child might be reading a story about a boat trip when they come across the unfamiliar and irregularly spelled word 'yacht'. Most children of six or above will be able to identify the first and last letters of this word ('y' and 't') but will struggle with decoding the middle letters 'ach'. A teacher or parent might ask the child to sound out the word as far as they can and then to 'guess' at what it says by using the boating content of the story and perhaps also where the word appears in the sentence. Children who have a good vocabulary should be able to work out that the word that they are struggling to decode is very probably 'yacht'.

LET'S RECAP

- Phonological (or auditory working) memory reflects how efficiently we code words in our short-term memory store. Measured by tasks such as repeating digit strings, it has an influence on reading development.
- Naming speed (of letters, colours etc.) appears to capture how easily we can retrieve words from our long-term memory, and is strongly related to speed of reading and spelling skills.
- Phonological skills have a powerful and long-term influence over reading development; this suggests that early measures of phoneme awareness and phonological processing might be used to screen children who are at risk of reading difficulties.
- When children come to read more complex texts, they use their vocabulary knowledge and their

> understanding of grammar to draw on context and
> content clues that make it easier for them to read
> difficult words.

The learning environment is important too!
Is learning to read different in other languages?

We live in a multicultural society, so as a teacher you may well
have a number of children in your class for whom English is not
their mother tongue, with these children growing up surrounded
by more than one language. You may be asking yourself, does that
complicate the picture? A child may have started learning to talk
in a foreign language and only come to learning English when they
started nursery school. Would we expect that to make a difference
as to how easily they learn to read?

Much of the research into reading and its relation to phonology
has been carried out in the English language. English is a much
harder language in which to learn to read, write and spell than, for
instance, Spanish, Italian or German. Languages such as Spanish and
Italian are described as **phonologically transparent**, which means
that there is a high level of consistency in their spelling patterns;
when you hear a specific sound in, for instance, Spanish, it is almost
always spelled with the same letter sequence, irrespective of the
word in which it appears. English has a **complex morpho-phono-
logical** structure which means that it is based on both morphemes
(units of meaning) as well as phonemes (units of sound). When
spelling in English, it is not unusual for the morphemic root to be
retained even at the expense of phonology. For instance, when asked
to spell the word 'healthy', the young child might be tempted to spell
the word phonically, thus writing 'helthy'. However, the root word of
'healthy' is 'heal' and it is this morphemic root that is retained when
spelling 'healthy', making it seemingly irregular in its spelling. There
are many English spellings like this which can present a significant
challenge for young children. Also, many of the commonest words in
the English language do not obviously conform to standard phono-
logical-based pronunciations – words like 'was', 'because', 'one', 'are'

and 'said'. Moreover, the same sound in English may be represented in print by a number of different letter combinations; for instance, the sound 'ee' can be written as 'ee' as in 'meet', 'ea' as in 'seat', or 'ei' as in 'receipt'.

English is a hard language to read in – the evidence

The language in which a child is taught to read is a factor that can affect ease of learning to read. This is nicely demonstrated in a study carried out by Philip Seymour (2005), who traced early literacy development over three years in English-speaking and Finnish-speaking children. He wanted to determine how much easier it is to learn to read in a highly phonologically transparent language like Finnish than in a non-phonologically transparent language like English. He found that it took the English-speaking children two years to learn to read to an agreed reading standard, in contrast to the Finnish speaking children who took only one year to reach the same standard (even after taking into account the different ages at which children start to learn to read in these countries).

But the foundations are the same

Whether a child is learning English, French or Spanish, it seems that reading is based on the same early foundation skills. This was nicely demonstrated in a study of learning to read in different languages conducted by Mai keta Caravolas and her colleagues in 2012. They followed the reading development of children from age five to eight who were learning to read in a range of different European languages, varying in transparency from non-transparent (e.g. English) through to largely transparent (e.g. Croatian). They found that early phonological awareness, emerging letter knowledge and rapid letter naming predicted later reading development in **all** of the languages. This clearly demonstrates that alphabetic reading systems are built on the same early foundations, regardless of how transparent or not they are.

Parents influence their children's reading development too!

Phonological skill and alphabet learning are **cognitive** predictors of learning to read. However, there are also environmental factors that influence children's progress in learning to read. These enable us to put together a more complete picture of how children learn

43

to read in an environmental or cultural context. Culture influences the values that families place on reading and writing. Middle-class and well-educated families value literacy skills highly because of the important role they play in enabling their child to achieve academic success. In contrast, gypsy or traveller communities have oral traditions that are stronger than written traditions. And we have just seen that the language in which a given child learns to read is also a cultural factor that predicts ease of learning to read, though it is not one that we can easily control or alter.

An important environmental factor that affects children's reading is the role that parents can play in helping their child learn to read; psychologists sometimes refer to this as the **home literacy environment**. Research studies have shown that, first, parents reading story books to their children influences their oral language skill, growth in spoken vocabulary knowledge and some pre-literacy skills (which would include children's awareness of books and print, and their emerging letter knowledge). Second, the more often parents read to their children the more advanced is their oral language.

How parents can make shared reading most effective

In general, parents reading story books to their children helps develop their oral language skills but not usually their reading. But if parents make an effort to draw their children's attention to printed words, letters and sounds in the stories they are reading to them, then the child's reading is improved too. So for instance a parent might:

- point to, while pronouncing, common printed words like 'mum', 'cat' or 'the'
- draw their children's attention to initial letters in printed words and then tell them how to say the sound, for example, 'Here's the word "sat"; the first letter in this word is "s" and it makes the "ss" sound'
- ask their child to come up with other words that begin with the same letter or sound of the word just read, for example, 'Here's the word "sat" that begins with the "ss" sound. Can you think of other words that begin with the "ss" sound?'

44

Reaching all families to help their child get off to a good start

Bookstart is a UK-based government-funded national scheme that aims to foster reading experiences in the pre-school years via the Health Visiting Service. Books and related materials are supplied free of charge to all families when their children are aged eight months, eighteen months, three years and four to five years. The children's books are accompanied by parent guidelines which recommend how parents should use these books to promote their children's enjoyment of stories, their awareness of printed words, their vocabulary knowledge and their familiarity with letters and numbers. It is hoped that the Bookstart scheme will help to 'even the playing field' for those children from disadvantaged backgrounds who do not automatically have the same access to books and related materials enjoyed by children from more advantaged homes. Despite the wide availability of Bookstart materials, the charity BookTrust estimated in a survey (Bookstart, 2014) that only 24 per cent of parents find the time to regularly read their child a bedtime story – a disappointing statistic, given that we have seen that shared book reading helps develop children's oral language development and possibly (less directly) their emerging literacy skills.

And school is the most important environmental factor of all!

Children learn to read at school. It follows that the amount of attention paid to teaching reading in the classroom and the quality of that teaching are crucial to ensuring that children learn to read to the level that enables them to access comfortably their school curriculum. This is, of course, where you as a classroom teacher come in. The scientific evidence that supports the most effective teaching methods will be covered in depth in Part 2 of the book when I address practical issues around teaching. For children who find it hard to learn to read, the quantity and quality of their literacy instruction is even more critical. Again, we will look at what teaching methods work best for children with literacy difficulties in Part 2.

LET'S RECAP

- English is a much harder language to learn to read in than, for instance, Spanish because of its complex spelling – though the foundations of literacy are the same for all languages.
- Parents who regularly read stories to their children help their oral language development, and if they draw their children's attention to letters and sounds in the stories, their literacy skills will also improve.
- The extent to which literacy teaching is emphasized in the classroom and the quality of that teaching substantially influences children's progress in learning to read.

What skills are needed for reading comprehension?

The answer to this question comes from an important model of reading comprehension called the Simple View of Reading Comprehension. The Simple View sees reading comprehension (or reading for meaning) as determined by just two component skills: reading accuracy and listening comprehension. Reading accuracy can be measured by a single-word reading test or a test of story reading accuracy. Listening comprehension is a term used to describe children's ability to understand language in spoken form; this is dependent on the child's level of oral language skill. The listening comprehension component of the Simple View can be measured in a number of different ways, including asking children to repeat orally a story that has been read to them, and also through tests of verbal intelligence, vocabulary knowledge and grammar. The general consensus is that it doesn't really matter which measures of reading accuracy and listening comprehension are used, as together they explain the entire process of reading for meaning.

How we proved this model works

Our longitudinal study I described earlier provides clear evidence for the Simple View of Reading Comprehension (Muter *et al.*, 2004). When the children were aged five, they were given tests not only of phonological awareness, letter knowledge and word reading but also tests of **vocabulary** knowledge and **grammar** (like awareness of past tense word endings and whether children could recognize if words in a spoken sentence were in the right order or not). The vocabulary and grammar tests assessed the children's oral language skills which is the listening comprehension component in our reading comprehension model.

One year later, when the children were aged six, they were asked to read out loud a story to the examiner who then asked them (orally) questions about the content of what they had read. This test provided us with measures of reading accuracy and, importantly, reading comprehension. We were able to show that the children's scores on the vocabulary and grammar knowledge tests given at age five predicted their reading comprehension scores at age six. This was in addition to the contribution made by reading accuracy at age five to reading comprehension a year later. Together, reading accuracy, vocabulary and grammar knowledge assessed at age five accounted for (or explained) almost all of the children's reading comprehension skills a year later. These results are exactly in line with what we know from the Simple View of Reading Comprehension.

Some additional facts about reading comprehension

The Simple View is a very robust model. Children who read text accurately and who have good oral language skills (the two components of the Simple View) will be good at comprehending what they read. In contrast, children who struggle with reading words accurately and/or whose oral language skills are weak could well find comprehending text a challenge. Some recent research studies have added further information to this model:

- First, vocabulary knowledge has an especially important role to play in reading comprehension.
- Second, while word reading accuracy and listening comprehension are both important to reading comprehension in the early school years, the impact of reading accuracy on comprehension lessens as children get older. As most children can read pretty accurately by

the end of primary school, it is only variations in their oral language skill that can influence reading comprehension. So oral language skills become the driving force in the development of children's reading comprehension during their secondary school years.

LET'S RECAP

- The ability to read for meaning (reading comprehension) is determined by just two component skills – listening comprehension (an oral language skill) and the accuracy with which children can read text.
- Vocabulary knowledge plays a very important role in reading comprehension and this is especially true of the secondary school years.

Let's conclude our discussion of reading comprehension by relating the Simple View of Reading Comprehension to how comprehension skills are taught in the classroom (see Box 2.1 below). In this example, reading for meaning is seen as an important literacy skill to be taught in its own right during the course of Year 2 after children have developed core word level reading skills.

Box 2.1: Linking the simple view of reading comprehension to classroom teaching practice in Year 2

In this example, a Year 2 teacher has set up reading comprehension lessons that use carpet time, desk activities and reading time to develop these skills.

Carpet time

At the beginning of Year 2, the teacher works on developing the **children's listening comprehension skills**. She reads a story book to the class and then talks to them about it. She asks some of the children to repeat back to her chunks of the story by, for instance, asking: 'Who can tell me who's

---

in this story?', 'Where is it happening?', 'How does the story begin?', 'What happens next?', 'How does it all end?' Or she might ask them specific questions about the content (e.g. 'What colour dress was Rachel wearing?') or even ask them questions that mean they have to infer or 'read between the lines' (e.g. 'Why do you think Freddie got so cross?', 'What could happen next?'). From time to time, the teacher talks about words in the text that the children might not have come across before – she tells them what the words mean and how they are used, so helping the children develop a wider vocabulary. Each child goes home from school every week with a new book; the teacher writes in their homework book that the parents should read the book out loud to their child and then get them to talk about the story.

Later on in Year 2, the teacher moves on to **reading comprehension**. Now the children read the printed story from the whiteboard silently to themselves. After they've all finished reading it, she asks them to 'tell it back' or to answer questions she puts to them about the story content. She talks about new and difficult words they might not know so that with practice they can add them to their vocabularies. The children take a book home every week to read to their parents, who ask them to tell the story in their own words and answer questions about what they've read.

The teacher (or the class teaching assistant) spends time with each child on their own twice a week, listening to them read. She asks each child to repeat the stories they have just read in their own words, then answer questions about their understanding of what they have read. The teacher checks that the child knows what new and difficult words mean.

Desk activities

In the middle and end of Year 2, after carpet-time reading comprehension work, the children go to their desks to do independent reading comprehension activities that now include writing. The children read silently to themselves a story that is presented on the whiteboard or from a book or photocopied sheet. The teacher then puts up on the white-board a set of comprehension questions based on the story, and the children have to read the questions and write down their answers in their exercise book. The teacher and the class's teaching assistant walk among the groups, helping children who are finding this hard. Every week, the children take a new book home to read and the teacher writes in the homework book the comprehension questions they have to answer and write down in their exercise book.

KEY MESSAGES TO TAKE AWAY

✓ Good phonological processing (phonological memory/auditory working memory and naming speed) is needed for children to access phonological representations of words in their memory store – which especially impacts their reading speed and their spelling.

✓ Phonological awareness and processing speed tests are good long-term predictors of reading achievement; might they form the basis for developing screening measures that identify young children at risk of reading difficulties?

✓ As children read more complex books, oral language skills (like vocabulary and grammar) play an increasingly important role, helping children make use of context and content clues in text to read an unfamiliar word that they might not recognize if it were on its own.

✓ Environmental factors important to reading include the language in which the child is learning to read (English is a particularly hard language to read), parents reading story books to their children (which helps develop their oral language and early reading skills) and the extent to which the teaching of reading is emphasized in the classroom and the quality of that teaching.

✓ Reading comprehension is determined by just two component skills – reading accuracy and listening comprehension – with oral language skills playing an increasingly important role in reading for meaning as children get older.

Chapter 3

When Literacy Development Goes Wrong

Dyslexia and Reading Comprehension Difficulties

In this chapter I describe how:

→ we define dyslexia as a word-level reading difficulty that affects children's reading accuracy, reading speed and spelling
→ dyslexia is seen as an inherited difficulty which affects the way the brain is wired
→ the phonological deficit theory of dyslexia is a way of explaining how a dyslexic child's underlying phonological difficulties affect their ability to learn phonics, a key skill needed to learn to read and spell
→ artificial intelligence models describe the dyslexic child's phonological hardware as 'disrupted' so they cannot form mapping (or connections) between sounds and letters
→ dyslexia first affects learning the letters of the alphabet, then impacts the ability to read accurately and most usually leads to long-term difficulties in reading speed and spelling
→ children with reading comprehension problems have underlying oral language difficulties which may affect their educational progress long term.

In the previous two chapters, we saw that phonological abilities have a powerful impact on children's early reading development. Children who find analysing sounds in words easy tend to be good readers while children who struggle with this skill seem to find reading hard. Could a weakness in phonological ability explain the word-level reading difficulties we see in children who are described as having dyslexia? Answering this question will be the main focus of this chapter. We will also look later on at the difficulties experienced by children who find it hard to comprehend what they read.

How do we define dyslexia?

The term 'dyslexia' has a long and quite controversial history. Let's start by looking at a widely accepted definition of dyslexia which, though admittedly rather old, still holds up well – and provides clues about the causes of this learning difficulty. Professor Margaret Snowling wrote in 2000: 'dyslexia is a specific form of language impairment that affects the way the brain encodes phonological features of spoken words; it specifically affects the development of reading and spelling, and its effects can be modified through development leading to various behavioural manifestations' (pp.213–214). I'll try to unpick this definition a little. Professor Snowling starts by pointing out that dyslexia is brain based; this means that it is a difficulty caused by dysfunctional genes which in turn affect the way the brain is wired. She then goes on to describe the underlying learning (cognitive) difficulty that the child with dyslexia has – specifically a deficit or weakness in the phonological processing component of language. It is this phonological difficulty that causes the reading and spelling problems experienced by the child with dyslexia. Although Professor Snowling views dyslexia as brain based, she very much makes the point that reading and spelling difficulties can present differently from one child to the next and can be impacted by environmental factors, including parental influences and the effects of teaching.

Two recent controversies around dyslexia

The first controversy is about 'deficits' versus 'differences'. Psychologists view dyslexia and other specific learning difficulties as being caused by a deficit in an underlying skill or ability. However, there has been a recent move to replace the term 'deficit' with 'difference', which of course carries a less negative connotation, so dyslexia is seen as a normal difference in the way people learn.

This **neurodiversity model** states that the differences or diversities of minds and brains should be valued not denigrated; terms like 'disability', 'deficit' and 'disorder' are considered stigmatizing and should be avoided. Disability is seen as something that is imposed on top of an individual's impairment that isolates and excludes them from society. It follows that people need not be disabled if the infrastructure around them is modified so as to accommodate for their difficulties in such a way that barriers to opportunity are reduced. In my view, labelling an individual 'neurodiverse' is not helpful as it is too vague a description; we need to specify in **what way the individual is neurodiverse** – that is, whether they have literacy difficulties, language problems, attention difficulties and so on.

In relation to dyslexia, the neurodiversity model emphasizes setting in place inclusion services, accommodations such as extra time in exams, using assistive technologies and providing support and mentoring. Providing accommodations and supports for children with literacy difficulties is essential, but the problem with the neurodiversity approach is that it tends to underplay the difficulties an individual has that can and should be remediated (or treated). In this chapter, I explore the evidence that dyslexic children are not just different but have underlying deficits in skills that are essential to normal literacy development. These in turn create very real barriers to children accessing their school curriculum, which in turn prevents them from fulfilling their potential and results in restricted opportunities that often continue into adulthood – and may impact their mental health. Providing support and accommodations is in my view half the answer. Ameliorating children's literacy difficulties through special teaching is the other half! This book addresses both.

The second controversy centres around whether dyslexia exists at all. Julian Elliott and Elena Grigorenko (2014), in their book *The Dyslexia Debate*, deny that dyslexia is a valid diagnosis. They argue that it is not possible to separate poor readers into clear causal groups, based on their having a particular learning difficulty such as a phonological weakness. Additionally, they deny that we can identify a special group of children we call 'dyslexic' within a larger pool of poor readers. (We do need to keep in mind that environmental factors such as poor school attendance or inadequate teaching may be sufficient to explain why some children have reading problems.) Elliot and Grigorenko appear to particularly object to the so-called vast dyslexia industry which provides assessments and special help that middle-class families can afford while less advantaged families cannot. The authors conclude their case by calling for an end to the dyslexia label. They suggest that it be replaced simply by a description of the particular difficulties that a given child has. Personally, I do not think it matters whether we describe an individual child's reading difficulty as dyslexia or a specific reading problem or a literacy disorder/difficulty. What is important is to have an understanding of what that child's difficulties are and how we should teach them so as to improve their literacy skills. There is now increased agreement that the term 'dyslexia' (or literacy difficulty, if preferred) should be reserved for children who have persisting reading problems and who have proved slow to respond to good teaching and extra help.

Creating a model of the causes of dyslexia

Returning to Professor Snowling's definition of dyslexia, we can build a model that is a useful framework for studying the causes of dyslexia (see Figure 3.1). This model sets out three different levels of study that create a causal pathway: the **biological**, the **cognitive** and the **behavioural**. It also recognizes that environmental factors can influence this pathway.

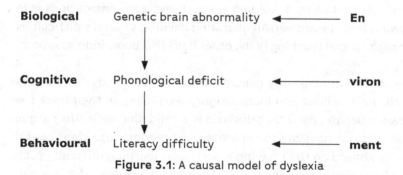

Figure 3.1: A causal model of dyslexia

At the uppermost level of the model is the **biological** basis of dyslexia; there is good evidence to show that dyslexia is caused by dysfunctional genes that in turn affect how the brain functions.

At the next level, the brain dysfunction leads to a **cognitive** (specifically a phonological) weakness which then leads to the **behavioural** expression of dyslexia, namely that of difficulty in learning to read and spell.

Environmental factors that feed into this causal pathway might include social and family factors, the language in which the child is learning to read (see Chapter 2) and quality of teaching.

Dyslexia is a brain-based difficulty
WHAT GENETIC RESEARCH TELLS US
It has been known for a long time that dyslexia 'runs in families', which suggests that it is a strongly inherited learning difficulty. Family at-risk studies look at the learning profiles of young children who have a first degree relative (usually a parent) who is known to have dyslexia. These studies have shown that there is a 45 per cent chance of a child developing reading difficulties if one of their parents is found to have dyslexia. This is much higher than the incidence of dyslexia in the general population which is around 5–8 per cent.

Genetic studies have shown that reading skills are quite strongly inherited. However, environmental factors are important too. Phonological awareness, a cognitive skill, is highly heritable, so genes seem to be more important than environment during the first two to three years of learning to read (we saw in Chapter 1 that phonological awareness has a huge influence on beginning reading). However, environmental factors appear to be more important than genetic factors in the pre-school years because parents reading to their children plays an important role, and then again in the late primary and secondary school years when classroom teaching and teenagers' reading preferences make a big contribution. Scientists are now beginning to identify specific genes that are associated with having dyslexia.

THE DYSLEXIC BRAIN IS DIFFERENT
Alongside the genetic basis of dyslexia, there are studies that look at brain function in dyslexic children and adults. We have seen that language abilities (in particular phonological aspects

of language) affect how easily children learn to read and spell. It follows therefore that the brain regions we know to be responsible for language and phonological skills might not function as they should in people with dyslexia. Research has shown us that as children develop, language skills become increasingly localised or 'fixed' in the left side of the brain. We can study how the brain works using medical technology such as brain scans that measure patterns of brain activation; the amount of activation in a given brain region tells us how well that region is functioning. When brain activation is measured in dyslexic people who are carrying out reading or phonological tasks, they show decreased activity in the left-side language areas of the brain (while normal readers show increased brain activation in these areas).

LET'S RECAP

- Dyslexia is a specific learning difficulty that is associated with underlying language (mainly phonological) difficulties that impair children's ability to learn to read and spell.
- Dyslexia is strongly inherited but environmental experiences also play a role in how the child's literacy difficulty is expressed.
- People with dyslexia show under-activation in the specialized language (and phonological) areas of the left side of the brain.

From brain to cognition in dyslexia

The **phonological deficit theory of dyslexia** views weak phonological skills as the main cause of reading difficulties. There are hundreds of published research studies that support the theory that dyslexic children have poorly developed phonological skills. Many have shown that dyslexic children find phonological awareness tasks (like deleting sounds from spoken words) much more difficult than children of the same age who are normal readers; dyslexic children even find tasks like this harder than children who are younger than them but who read at the same low level. Also,

56

studies have shown that dyslexic children are poor phonological processors so they struggle with tasks of naming speed, phonological/auditory working memory and non-word repetition. In general, we find that the more severe the phonological deficit in dyslexic children the more severe the reading difficulty.

Dyslexic children show a phonological deficit even before they learn to read. Family at-risk studies which study children born into dyslexic families demonstrate this clearly. Snowling, Gallagher and Frith (2003) followed 56 such children at high risk of reading difficulties from just before their fourth birthday until they were eight years of age. The children who went on to develop dyslexia (they were poor readers at age eight), had shown delayed speech and language development at three years nine months. They also showed weaknesses in phonological awareness, naming objects at speed, emerging letter knowledge and non-word repetition. This is clear evidence that the phonological deficit is there even before the reading difficulty becomes evident – which implies that delayed phonological development is the likely cause of a dyslexic-based reading difficulty.

LET'S RECAP

- The phonological deficit theory of dyslexia views the literacy difficulties experienced by dyslexic children as being caused by a weakness in their phonological abilities.
- The more severe the phonological deficit, the more severe the reading difficulty.
- The phonological deficit is evident in dyslexic children before they learn to read.

From the evidence I've presented, it is tempting to feel confident that the cause of dyslexia has been established once and for all. However, we will see in the next two chapters that this theory turns out to be rather simplistic and does eventually fail to explain a lot of what we know about dyslexic children.

From cognition to behaviour in dyslexia

The third level of study in our causal model of dyslexia is the behavioural level which is the level at which the dyslexia is expressed educationally. In effect we can ask, how does a deficit in phonological skill affect children's reading and spelling? Let's try to answer this question by revisiting the computer-based artificial intelligence model of reading that we looked at in relation to typical literacy development in Chapter 1.

In our computer model, the differences between the typical reader and the reader with dyslexia are shown in the following diagram (Figure 3.2).

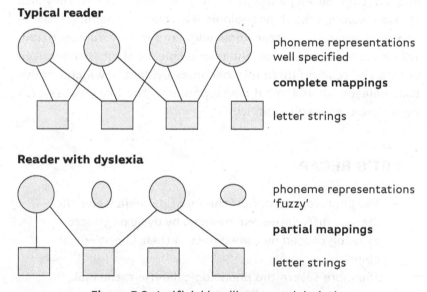

Figure 3.2: Artificial intelligence and dyslexia

Phonological awareness and processing tasks measure the strength of children's **phoneme representations** – that is, how strongly their knowledge of word sounds is stored in their long-term memory. In the good reader, phoneme representations are clear and strong so that when the child is presented with a new word to read, it is easy for them to create complete and accurate mappings (or connections) between the sounds the word makes and its printed letter string. This means that the word is read correctly even after the child has seen it just a few times.

In contrast, the dyslexic child has phoneme representations that are 'fuzzy' and weak (i.e. their phonological hardware is disrupted). These disrupted phoneme representations prevent the development of complete and accurate mappings between sounds and letters. So, when the child with dyslexia has to read a new word they are able to achieve only partial (or incomplete) mappings between sounds and letters; and even after they have seen the word many times, they may still read it incorrectly. Many parents and teachers note that the dyslexic child finds it hard to read a given word even though it may reappear over and over again in the books they read. Having said that, some dyslexic children can still manage to read accurately (especially story books) on the basis of partial letter-sound mappings. What they do is to 'fill the gaps' by making use of the story content, or by relying on the context in which the word appears or its position in the sentence. You might recall the example I gave in Chapter 2 where a child comes across the unfamiliar word 'yacht' in a story about boating. They can manage to identify the first and last letters, 'y' and 't' – that is, they show partial sound-to-letter mappings of the word. They are then able to work out that the word must be 'yacht' because of the content of the boating story and the context in which the word occurs.

Most dyslexic children find spelling even more difficult than reading. This is because full and complete letter-sound mappings are necessary for a word to be spelled correctly – and unfortunately, relying on context does not help at all with spelling.

How dyslexia shows differently over time

One of the first signs of dyslexia is slowness in learning the names and sounds of the 26 letters of the alphabet during the first year at school. Children with dyslexia cannot easily learn the letters of the alphabet because the mappings between sounds and letters are incomplete and insecure.

The dyslexic child's difficulty in mapping letters to speech sounds means that they find it hard to develop phonic-based (decoding) reading strategies – which they need to do by the time they are in Year 1. One direct way of measuring a child's level of phonic skill is to ask them to attempt to read nonsense words, words that they have never seen before (since they don't exist), nor which have any meaning. These 'made-up' non-words can be read only if the child is able to apply sound-to-letter mapping rules in a systematic way. There is a great deal of evidence that dyslexic children have considerable difficulty in reading non-words like 'fup', 'stip' and 'bolrik'. Studies of non-word reading in dyslexic children have shown that not only do they have difficulties in decoding non-words when compared to same-age good readers, their non-word reading is often poorer than that of younger children who are reading at the same level as them. Children with the most severe phonological deficits have the most difficulty reading non-words. As we shall see in later chapters, the use of non-word reading tests as an assessment tool is of enormous value in 'diagnosing' dyslexia and also in determining how severe the child's phonic decoding difficulties are.

How dyslexia presents may change over the course of development. Dyslexia can look very different at one stage of development than another. A child identified with dyslexia at age seven may present very differently by the time they are 16. Dyslexic children who receive good literacy instruction, preferably as early as possible and for as long as needed, may well overcome the worst of their reading difficulties by the time they are adolescents. How dyslexia presents in the teen years and in adulthood can be affected not only by the dyslexic person's learning experiences but also by their ability to draw on their personal strengths to help mitigate their difficulties. For example, the verbally able child can learn to draw on their good language skills and the context clues available in the stories they read which can help them read words they cannot identify singly and out of context.

Dyslexic children who have mild phonological weaknesses can, after a late start, learn to read adequately by the time they start secondary school but they are likely to have continuing spelling difficulties. In dyslexic children with severe phonological difficulties (especially those who do not receive the right kind of teaching), the educational gap between them and their classmates often widens as they get older. Attention- and frustration-based behaviour problems may develop and their oral language development (especially their vocabulary knowledge) slows down due to their avoidance of reading books. People with severe dyslexia usually have marked reading speed and spelling difficulties that persist into adulthood – which may in turn affect their ability to pass exams, obtain qualifications and succeed in their work life without access to proper support.

LET'S RECAP

- Dyslexic children find it hard to form strong connections (or mappings) between sounds and printed letters, which makes it difficult for them to learn the alphabet and to use phonic decoding strategies.
- Dyslexic children may present very differently at different ages, depending on the severity of their difficulties and the learning experiences they have.

The phonology–decoding–reading disconnection: The case of Nicholas

We will now look at a (mostly) true case study–though with the name changed–that illustrates the strength of the phonology–decoding–reading connection (or perhaps more accurately **disconnection**) in the child with dyslexia. I also show in this example how dyslexia presents over the course of a child's primary schooling. Nicholas was a participant (along with 37 other children) in one of my longitudinal studies (Muter *et al.*, 1998). There was no indication at the outset of this study that Nicholas would go on to develop severe dyslexia.

● NICHOLAS

Nicholas was first seen at age four during his last term at nursery school before he had started to learn to read. He was a bright and chatty little boy, enthusiastic, sociable and eager to please. He had not as yet established phonological or letter knowledge skills but then nor had his classmates.

Nicholas was seen again two years later at age six as he approached the end of Year 1. During those two years, his class-mates made good progress in their phonological awareness, as shown in their performance on a beginning sound deletion task (e.g. 'cat' without the 'c' says...? (response: 'at')). By the end of Year 1, the average score for the group as a whole was five (out of ten items), while Nicholas was unable to score at all. By the end of Year 1, he was able to identify only five letters of the alphabet while the average for the group was 19. It was clear that he was not developing the skills necessary for learning to read, and more specifically to acquire the alphabetic principle we talked about in Chapter 1. He performed poorly on a single-word reading test at the end of Year 1 (he was able to read five words accurately from the reading list, while the group average was 17). His struggle to acquire phonic skills was clearly demonstrated by his inability to read simple non-words, in contrast to many of his classmates who were now beginning to develop this skill. Interestingly, he performed well in line with his classmates on an arithmetic test. It was evident by age six that Nicholas had the learning profile we would expect to see in a child with emerging dyslexia. His teachers were told about our concerns, though we were unsure as to how much additional help he went on to receive.

We had the opportunity to follow up this sample of children when they were aged ten and in their penultimate year at primary school. Nicholas, along with 33 other children, returned to the study. Nicholas continued to display significant difficulties with phonological awareness, phonic decoding and literacy, with the performance gap between him and his classmates appearing ever larger. On a phonological awareness test of 24 items which required the children to delete a specified sound from a spoken non-word in order to come up with a real word (e.g. 'stip' without the 't' says 'sip'), Nicholas obtained a score of only four, while the group average was 17. He was still very poor at decoding, as shown by his score of only two (out of 20) on a one- and two-syllable non-word reading test, in contrast to the group average score of 14–15. His reading and spelling were very poor indeed; he scored in the bottom 5 per cent for his age group on standardized tests of reading and spelling. See Figure 3.3 for a sample of Nicholas's poor spelling and writing. Interestingly, his score on a maths test was within the normal range.

Not only was Nicholas struggling in literacy, but he scored within the 'clinical problem range' on behaviour checklists completed by his parents and teachers. He had gone from being a happy, well-behaved four-year-old at the beginning of the study to a disengaged, unhappy, anxious and defensive ten-year-old by the time the study was completed.

Nicholas's case clearly demonstrates the strong association between phonological skills and learning to read. His difficulties with phonology and learning to read that were seen at age six were still there at age ten. On a practical note, our case study suggests that, first, children at risk of dyslexia can be identified at an early age, as young as five or six (through giving them simple tests of phonological ability and letter knowledge). Second, it follows that dyslexic children should have special literacy teaching from an early age and for as long as needed at primary school; this ensures that they not only make progress in reading and spelling, but, equally as important, their likely deteriorating motivation and behaviour might be prevented.

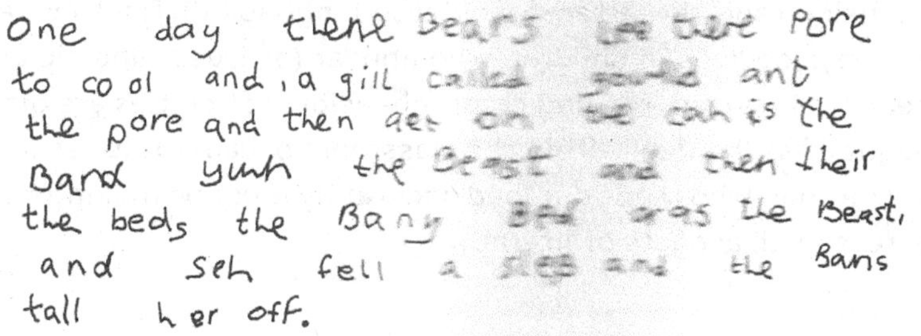

One day thene Dears ... were Pore to co ol and , a gill ca ... ant the pore and then ae on ... cah is the Bard yunh the Beast ... then their the beds the Bany ... was the Beast, and Seh fell a ... the Bans tall h er off.

Figure 3.3: A sample of Nicholas's writing

Reading comprehension difficulties

In Chapter 2, we saw that reading comprehension is the product of two component skills: word reading accuracy and listening comprehension. In this Simple View of Reading Comprehension, it would be reasonable to expect that if a child is struggling to comprehend what they read, they must have a difficulty either with reading the text accurately or with processing the language information contained in that text – or perhaps even both.

Defining reading comprehension difficulties

Children with reading comprehension difficulties are those whose reading comprehension skills are far worse than expected from their level of reading accuracy. We can demonstrate this by, for instance, giving the child a test that requires them to read a piece of text out loud and then answer questions about its content. We record the reading errors they make while they read the text and we time how long it takes them to read it. We then come up with measures of reading accuracy and reading speed. After the child has read the passage, they are asked questions which assess their understanding of what they have read. A reading comprehension score is obtained which can then be compared to the child's reading accuracy and speed scores. Many children with dyslexia (especially if they have good language skills) will score reasonably well on the reading comprehension measure, but obtain low scores for reading accuracy and speed. In contrast, the child with a reading comprehension difficulty will read the text accurately and even fluently, but fail to comprehend what they have read.

It has been estimated that as many as 10 per cent of our child population has a reading comprehension difficulty. Reading comprehension (and the often-associated language difficulties) are not always obvious in children who appear (at least superficially) to read well. Indeed, reading comprehension difficulties are often thought of as 'hidden' within the classroom because it is assumed that the child who reads out loud accurately must be making good progress in all aspects of literacy.

What do we know about children with reading comprehension difficulties?

- Children with reading comprehension difficulties show problems with the listening comprehension component of the Simple View Model. They display a wide range of **oral language difficulties**, including having limited vocabulary knowledge, poor understanding of grammar and difficulties in understanding and also producing lengthy and complex spoken sentences. Children with reading comprehension difficulties have been shown to have oral language problems from an early age, which suggests that weak oral language is a **cause** of the reading comprehension difficulties that may not become evident until much later.

- Many poor comprehenders struggle with understanding the order and structure contained in a piece of text – that is, understanding that stories have a beginning, middle and end, and that we use connective words like 'and', 'but' and 'therefore' to link components of a story together.

- Poor comprehenders find it hard to remember new vocabulary, and they have difficulties in working out the meanings of unfamiliar words from surrounding text. This in turn affects their ability to understand what they are reading because they do not know the meanings of the words contained in the text.

- Poor comprehenders have great difficulty making **inferences** (i.e. going beyond what is written and 'reading between the lines'). For instance, a text might state, 'The bonfire began to burn uncontrollably. Jan rushed to pick up the garden hose.' An inferential comprehension question might ask, 'Why did Jan pick up the garden hose?' The child needs to infer that Jan is planning to put out the fire by spraying water from the hose.

- Poor comprehenders show weak **comprehension monitoring**. This describes the child's ability to recognize whether or not they are understanding what they are reading. The good comprehender realizes when they don't understand what they are reading so they go back and re-read the text until it eventually makes sense. Poor comprehenders often fail to realize that they have 'lost the plot', and nor do they appear to be prepared to re-read what they have not understood.

- Having poor reading comprehension has a massive impact on educational learning. Poor comprehenders in their secondary years have been shown to achieve low scores on national tests of English, maths and science.

LET'S RECAP

- As many as 10 per cent of children are able to read accurately but cannot understand and remember what they read – they have a reading comprehension difficulty.
- Children with reading comprehension difficulties show underlying weaknesses in their oral language (including having a limited vocabulary knowledge).
- Having poor oral language and reading comprehension difficulties have a long-term damaging effect on children's educational functioning.

KEY MESSAGES TO TAKE AWAY

✓ When we talk about literacy difficulties, we need to distinguish between difficulties in word-level reading (which we call 'dyslexia') and in reading comprehension.

✓ The model of dyslexia we have looked at describes three different levels that create a causal pathway: from the biological (genetic/neurological) to the cognitive (phonological) and then on to the behavioural (literacy skills).

✓ Dyslexia is an inherited learning difficulty that affects those brain areas whose normal function is needed for learning to read; dyslexic people show reduced activation in the left-side brain areas we know to be important for the development of language and phonological skills.

✓ At the cognitive level, difficulties with phonological awareness and processing (seen in dyslexic children even before they begin to learn to read) are thought to be the main cause of dyslexia.

✓ The weak and disrupted phoneme representations of the child with dyslexia prevent them developing complete and secure mappings between the sounds a word makes and its printed letter string; this means that they cannot easily use phonic decoding strategies.

✓ Children with poor reading comprehension show a wide range of oral language difficulties which have a long-term disruptive effect on their educational progress and attainments.

Chapter 4

Not All Dyslexic Children Look the Same

How We Explain Individual Differences

In this chapter I describe how:

→ the phonological deficit model of dyslexia introduced in Chapter 3 is a single deficit model that is based on the view that there is one set of damaged genes and one dysfunctional part of the brain that make a child dyslexic

→ recent research has now shown us that the same set of genes can lead to different learning difficulties, and at least two or three brain regions are 'disconnected' in the child with dyslexia

→ a child is more likely to get a diagnosis of dyslexia if they have not one single (phonological) difficulty but rather multiple difficulties (or 'risks')

→ children with mild dyslexia have fewer risks than children with severe dyslexia – and often develop compensating strategies which help them overcome the worst of their difficulties

→ children with severe dyslexia have far more risks, and very often weaknesses in oral language as well as phonological difficulties.

The multi-level model that we looked at in the previous chapter views dyslexia as being caused by a single underlying difficulty in phonological processing; we call this the **single (phonological) deficit model of dyslexia**. It assumes that a single brain module (or region) is responsible for a specific cognitive function — so one module is for understanding language, another module is for speech and yet another for phonological processing. It also assumes that these modules operate independently of each other. This approach has been widely accepted for many decades (and still is to some extent); it has been hugely influential in directing both research and clinical/educational practice in the field of literacy difficulties.

However, in this chapter and the next we will see that this single deficit model ultimately fails to fully and comprehensively describe the difficulties experienced by most dyslexic children. It certainly has problems explaining why parents and teachers often ask the question — why do dyslexic children seem to look different one from the other? Is it because there are different types of dyslexia or could it be just that some children have more severe problems than others and that some have additional difficulties beyond their dyslexia? After you've read Chapters 4 and 5, you'll come to realize that it's more to do with severity and additional difficulties than there actually being different types of dyslexia.

Why the single deficit model fails at the biological level

Let us consider the biological level of explanation first. Because the multi-level model of dyslexia is modular based, it assumes that different sets of genes and separate brain regions underlie different learning difficulties. So, for instance, it is proposed that there is one set of genes that determines whether a child will have dyslexia and a different set of genes that determines whether they will have an arithmetic difficulty and so on. Similarly, the modular view states that disruption to a single specific brain region results in dyslexia while disruption to a different specific region results in an arithmetic difficulty. We are beginning to see, however, that neither genes nor the human brain work in this simple modular fashion.

Let's look at genes first

It is important to understand at the outset that genes do not cause dyslexia as such; rather they create **'risks'** for developing it. Being at risk for a particular learning difficulty means that a given child has an increased probability of developing that difficulty, but that it is by no means inevitable that they will do so. Specific genes have been identified which increase the risk of a child developing dyslexia – the more **risk genes** the child has, the more likely they will have dyslexia. Some genes are **shared** across disorders; so, the **same genes** could put a child at risk for both dyslexia and language difficulties. There are also **non-shared genes** that are specific to particular disorders; so for instance, there could be some genes that predispose a child only to dyslexia but not language disorder, while different genes might result in a child developing a language disorder but not dyslexia.

And now the brain

The single deficit model assumes that a given cognitive difficulty (such as phonological processing) is solely located in a specific isolated brain region – and nowhere else in the brain. However, brain scan studies have shown that cognitive functioning is determined partly by how well a particular brain region functions, but also by the **connections** that a brain region has with other regions. It is almost certain that we need two (maybe even three) brain regions to each be functioning well (and to work together) in order to learn to read. Recent research has shown us that there are **reduced connections** between the reading-related brain areas in people who are dyslexic (see Figure 4.1).

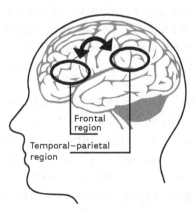

Figure 4.1: Connections between reading regions of the brain

LET'S RECAP

– The single (phonological) deficit model of dyslexia assumes that one set of genes causes dyslexia – but we now know that multiple sets of genes, some of which are shared across disorders, increase the risk of a child developing dyslexia.
– This model also assumes that dyslexia is caused by disruption to a single brain region – but research has shown us that at least two or three different brain regions are disrupted and disconnected in dyslexic people.

Why the single deficit model fails at the cognitive level

Not only does the single deficit model fail at the biological level, it also does so at the cognitive level. In this model, the dyslexic child's literacy difficulties are explained by their having a single under-lying phonological deficit (or difficulty). To demonstrate what is wrong with this view, it is helpful to look at the family at-risk study led by Margaret Snowling (2003) that I introduced in the previous chapter. This study began by selecting pre-school children from dyslexic families; these were the 'at-risk' children. At the same time, a control group was selected in which no child's parent or sibling was known to have reading difficulties. As expected, many more of the at-risk children (66 per cent) demonstrated signifi-cant literacy difficulties when they were followed up at age eight, compared with only 14 per cent of the controls.

The researchers also expected that the children in the at-risk group who were found to be struggling with reading at age eight (i.e. were dyslexic) would show difficulties with phonological tasks, while those in the at-risk group who did not have trouble read-ing (and were therefore not dyslexic) would have no difficulties with the phonological tasks. In other words, they were expect-ing an **all-or-none** outcome; if you had dyslexia you must have phonological difficulties, if you didn't have dyslexia you didn't have phonological difficulties. However, the results of the study did not show this to be the case. It was certainly true that those children in the at-risk group who had reading difficulties (**at-risk reading impaired**) struggled with the phonological tests. However, many of the at-risk children who were competent readers (and performing at a similar reading level to the controls) also found these phonological tasks hard. These children were described as **at-risk reading unimpaired**; they had a phonological deficit at the cognitive level but without the expected reading difficulties at the behavioural level. The researchers were forced to recognize that a single phonological deficit may not be sufficient to explain the reading difficulties experienced by children with dyslexia. Having said that, many of the at-risk reading unimpaired children, while reading words sufficiently well, nonetheless had spelling difficulties and their speed of reading was slow. We can conclude that dyslexia is not all-or-none; rather, it is a **dimensional** difficulty which occurs along a graded continuum that ranges from low risk through to high risk and from mild through to severe.

An important finding within the at-risk group was that the reading unimpaired children had much better oral language skills than the reading impaired children. It was suggested that at-risk children with good oral language skills may be able to 'get round' what should have been a reading difficulty by using compensatory strategies that protect them from reading failure. These children might be able to take advantage of context and content clues that are contained in text, while at the same time drawing on their good vocabulary knowledge. This means that they are better able to 'guess at' words that they cannot easily recognize out of context. In contrast, in this study, the reading impaired children were carrying two risk factors (a phonological deficit and poor oral language skills) which acted as **multiple risks** that increased the likelihood of their having reading difficulties.

LET'S RECAP

- The single deficit model of dyslexia makes an all-or-none prediction: if you have a phonological difficulty you must be a poor reader – but dyslexia is dimensional, not all-or-none (ranging from mild through to severe).

- Dyslexic children with very poor phonological skills who also have weak oral language will show a wide range of (often severe) literacy difficulties.
- However, dyslexic children with milder phonological difficulties, and especially those who have good oral language skills, may escape the worst of the reading problems, but will very likely struggle with spelling and speed of reading.

Which children develop dyslexia?

Whether a child develops dyslexia is determined by the number of risks (or deficits) they have. If a child has relatively few risks (perhaps even just one) and they have strengths that enable them to compensate for that risk, then they may not show literacy difficulties at all (or if they do, these are at a minor level). However, if a child is carrying **multiple risks**, there is an increased probability that these risks will build up to reach a critical threshold point that 'tips them over' into a dyslexic diagnosis.

What are the primary risks for dyslexia within our (new) **multiple deficit model**? We have already seen that being born into a family where there are other members who have literacy difficulties increases the risk that a child will develop dyslexia. What is the nature of that risk and are there associated and additional risks that make it likely that such a child will be diagnosed with dyslexia? We will now look at the important connection between early (pre-school) oral language difficulties and later emerging literacy difficulties. Before we do this, it is important to consider (albeit briefly) the characteristics of children who have a **developmental language disorder (DLD)** as this often overlaps with dyslexia.

There are three main features of DLD:

1. Children with DLD have difficulty in acquiring spoken language from the beginning; as pre-schoolers, they struggle to understand what others say to them and they find it hard to produce spoken language.
2. The language skills of children with DLD are well below the level expected for their age; the result is that they find it hard to communicate with other children, which affects them socially, and they also struggle at school because so much of learning in the classroom depends on understanding and using language correctly.
3. The language difficulties are not caused by hearing problems or medical or neurological conditions, and are not better explained by general slow learning (those children who are delayed in all aspects of their development, not just oral language).

More information about the nature of DLD is provided in Box 4.1.

Box 4.1: Developmental language disorder (DLD)

The term 'developmental language disorder' is used to describe children whose oral language skills are much poorer than their non-verbal (visual learning) abilities, which are usually within the normal range. Children with DLD make up quite a mixed group. Some children have difficulty with understanding and producing language (they have both a receptive and an expressive language disorder), others are able to understand spoken language but are unable to express themselves appropriately (expressive language disorder) and some children have accompanying speech problems which make their speech difficult for others to understand (speech sound disorder). Language disorders are seen in around 3–6 per cent of the child population, with boys more likely to be affected than girls.

Studies that have shown that 50 per cent of pre-schoolers with delayed language development go on to resolve their difficulties by the time they reach school age – that is, they 'catch up' in their language after a slow start – and many of these children will read normally. However, half the children presenting with language delay as pre-schoolers will have language difficulties that persist into middle childhood and beyond, which will in turn impair their educational progress and their social communication with others.

There are many theories about what causes language difficulties. Some claim that it is due to difficulty in developing knowledge of grammar, others suggest that it might arise from slow auditory processing, while still others emphasize difficulties with auditory working memory. Given the wide variation we see in DLD children, it is likely that we are looking at multiple cognitive difficulties that may affect separate components of language.

Over the last 10–15 years, Professors Margaret Snowling and Charles Hulme and their colleagues have carried out research studies that have enabled us to develop a better understanding of the relationship between early oral language weaknesses and later reading difficulties (Snowling *et al.*, 2016). These studies usually compare the oral language and literacy skills of children whose language is developing normally with those who have a particular learning difficulty – these will be children who have either dyslexia (on its own), oral language difficulties (again on their own) or **both** oral language and literacy difficulties. Many of these children come from families in which several members have literacy difficulties (i.e. they are at-risk children). I will now summarize the main findings of these studies and explain how these have improved our understanding of the experiences of children with language and literacy difficulties – and how these findings might point us in the direction of how we identify and help such children:

- Some studies have shown that there is a considerable overlap of dyslexia and language difficulties. Coming from a family of dyslexic people means that a child is more likely to have oral language, as well as literacy, difficulties. At a practical level, it has been suggested that screening pre-schoolers from families where dyslexia is present through giving them a phonological test (such as repeating nonsense words out loud), together with a broader language test (such as repeating long sentences out loud), might help teachers spot children at risk for language and later literacy difficulties.

- Having pre-school language difficulties and being born into a dyslexic family put a child at risk of developing dyslexia. However, an important point to bear in mind is that speech and language delay is not a good predictor of later reading difficulties until close to when children start school. This is in line with the view that many children with delayed language who resolve their difficulties by ages four to five years learn to read normally. In educational terms, it seems that **screening for dyslexia is unlikely to be reliable until close to school entry.** It has been suggested that good screening measures for dyslexia in the early school years would be alphabet letter knowledge and tests of phonological awareness and rapid naming.

- If a child's oral language difficulties persist into middle childhood, they are likely to experience educational difficulties; they need close monitoring during their primary school years as well as high levels of special teaching (and perhaps for some children even speech and language therapy).

- Children who have articulation difficulties (i.e. their speech is hard for others to understand) may have trouble with phonics and spelling after they start school. This is especially the case for children whose speech is **disordered** – that is, their speech does not follow the usual pattern of development, with often odd sound substitutions being present (which we don't see in normally developing children).

LET'S RECAP

- Children from dyslexic families are more likely to have oral language, as well as literacy, difficulties.
- A child with speech and language delay that has not resolved by the time they start school could develop reading difficulties later on.
- Screening measures that might spot dyslexic children in Year 1 include tests of phonological skill and letter knowledge.

Our first case study is Alex, whose history and presentation are described here. Alex's case illustrates how oral language and literacy skills are intimately related in the child with severe dyslexia and also describes how such a child might present in the classroom. His assessments and specialist teaching will be discussed in detail in Chapters 6 and 8.

CASE STUDY 1: ALEX, A LONG-TERM VIEW OF A CHILD WITH DEVELOPMENTAL LANGUAGE DISORDER (DLD) AND DYSLEXIA

Alex was referred to me for assessment at age six. His parents reported that he was a very late talker, and was in fact producing only single words at age two-and-a-half years. He underwent hearing tests which proved normal. At age three, Alex was referred for a speech and language assessment. This showed that his receptive and expressive language were both severely delayed. He went on to receive regular speech and language therapy up until the time he started school as a rising five-year-old. Alex found it difficult to settle into school life because of his poor understanding of spoken language and his struggles to express himself. He continued to receive speech and language therapy during his Reception class and Year 1. When he was referred to me for assessment, he was in Year 2 and making very slow educational progress, though he seemed to be a little stronger in maths than literacy. He was able to read and spell only a few simple and common words. There was a strong family history of reading and writing difficulties on his father's side of the family, including the father himself, who even as an adult was a very poor speller.

Alex's assessment at age six will be described in more detail in the later chapter on assessment. However, by way of summary, he demonstrated good, in fact above average, non-verbal abilities (he performed well on visual reasoning tasks like copying block patterns). When given a verbal ability test (oral tests of vocabulary knowledge and verbal reasoning), he scored at a below average level. On standardized tests of reading and spelling accuracy, he was achieving at the level of a typical five-year-old. His maths was noticeably stronger, and on an arithmetic test he scored at his age level. Alex's testing also showed that he had phonological/auditory working memory difficulties and poorly developed phonological awareness. It was concluded that Alex was a non-verbally able boy with a language difficulty who showed strong indicators for developing dyslexia.

Shortly after the assessment took place, Alex's parents and his school applied for an Education, Health and Care Plan (see Chapter 11), which provided speech and language therapy and special literacy teaching. However, he continued to struggle enormously within a mainstream school setting. At a review that took place when he was eight, it was decided that his educational needs would be better met in a special school setting. He was then placed at a school for children with language delays and difficulties, where he was able to receive high levels of speech and language therapy and one-to-one and small-group special education programmes delivered by specialist teachers. By age 11, it was decided that Alex had made sufficient progress for him to return to a mainstream school setting.

During Alex's secondary school years, he has been observed by his teachers to cope fairly well with the oral language demands of the classroom. However, his progress in terms of basic literacy is very much slower, even though he is continuing to receive additional learning support. Now aged 13 years, it is clear that he is struggling to make sense of his secondary school curriculum, hence this new referral for a further assessment. This second assessment is described in Chapter 6 when we will pick up Alex's story again.

KEY MESSAGES TO TAKE AWAY

✓ The single deficit model is based on the view that there is a specific set of damaged genes and one dysfunctional part of the brain that make a child dyslexic; however, we now know that genes can be shared across learning difficulties and that at least two or three brain regions are 'disconnected' in the dyslexic child.

✓ The single deficit model at the cognitive level assumes that dyslexia is all-or-none (you have dyslexia or you don't); however, evidence from at-risk studies shows that dyslexia ranges from mild through to severe, with its educational expression varying from child to child.

✓ Whether a given child develops dyslexia depends on the number of risks (or deficits) they have: the more risks a child has, the more likely these will build to reach a critical threshold that results in their being labelled dyslexic.

✓ A child is most at risk of developing severe dyslexia if they are born into a family where other members are poor readers and spellers, have pre-school speech and language difficulties which persist beyond the age of four to five years, have poor phonological skills, and are slow to learn the alphabet letters.

✓ The impact of risks can be reduced by the child having compensatory resources which may be part of their make-up (e.g. having good oral language skills), or through positive environmental experiences (e.g. early identification and intervention through screening of at-risk pre-schoolers).

Chapter 5

Why Many Dyslexic Children Have More Than Literacy Difficulties: Co-occurrence

In this chapter I describe how:

→ learning difficulties commonly co-occur which means that the child who has diagnosed dyslexia is likely to also have another separate learning difficulty – which could be an arithmetic problem, difficulties with attention or struggles with handwriting (and other motor skills)
→ two learning difficulties co-occur because they share genetic and cognitive risks (usually slow processing or early language delay), but there are also non-shared risks that are specific to particular learning difficulties
→ dyslexic children who also struggle with arithmetic often have early language and auditory working memory difficulties and may have a weak 'number sense'
→ dyslexic children who find it hard to concentrate have difficulties with controlling and inhibiting their behaviour and are usually slow and inefficient processors
→ dyslexic children who are also poor handwriters will typically have visual perceptual and motor difficulties.

There is good evidence that many children with one learning difficulty will also have another (different) learning difficulty – we call this 'co-occurrence'. There are two forms of co-occurrence:

• The first is when one learning difficulty is the **forerunner** of the other and pre-dates it; the overlap of dyslexia and language difficulties described in Chapter 4 is an example of this. In this form of co-occurrence, the language difficulty is obvious in the pre-school years but the reading difficulties are not evident until after the child starts school.

- The second form of co-occurrence is when two distinct learning difficulties co-exist at the same time; a good example of this would be dyslexia and co-occurring arithmetic disorder (or dyscalculia), which we see in school age children.

How do we account for co-occurrence?

One of my research studies (Snowling, Muter and Carroll, 2007) demonstrated that as many as seven in ten children who show a reading difficulty have additional difficulties in oral language, non-verbal/motor skills, attention control, arithmetic or, some-times, a combination of these. This means that dyslexic children have an increased likelihood of having co-occurring difficulties which are sometimes sufficiently severe to justify a formal diag-nosis of developmental language disorder (DLD), specific arithme-tic disorder/dyscalculia, attention deficit hyperactivity disorder (ADHD) or developmental coordination disorder (DCD)

At the genetic level, co-occurrence is explained by the concept of shared versus non-shared genes which I talked about in the previous chapter. To briefly recap, when genes are shared across learning difficulties it means that the same genes could lead to a child developing both dyslexia and, for instance, dyscalculia. Not only are genes shared across disorders but so also are cognitive difficulties (or deficits). This means that the same underlying learning difficulty can give rise to different disorders. For example, the same cognitive difficulty might predispose a child to develop dyslexia and also dyscalculia. It is this shared cognitive difficulty that explains why different disorders commonly overlap. However, there are also non-shared cognitive difficulties that are specific to different disorders – for example, a cognitive difficulty that gives rise to dyslexia but not dyscalculia and a different cognitive difficulty that gives rise to dyscalculia but not dyslexia. It is the non-shared difficulties that explain why there is not total overlap of two disorders.

One useful way of representing the co-occurrence of learning difficulties is in the form of a **Venn diagram**. I use these diagrams throughout the book because they display visually the co-occurrence of two disorders. They also relate this overlap to shared and non-shared difficulties that are evident at the cognitive through to the behavioural (educational) level. In the next section, I show what the Venn diagram for dyslexia and DLD looks like (Figure 5.1).

Later in this chapter, I illustrate how co-occurrence works for each of the simultaneous co-occurring difficulties (dyscalculia, ADHD and DCD) through three fictionalized case studies. These cases also show how a child who has dyslexia and a co-occurring difficulty would present in the classroom.

Dyslexia and co-occurring DLD

A disorder that frequently co-occurs with dyslexia is developmental language disorder (DLD), which I discussed in some depth in Chapter 4. Indeed, 50 per cent of children with pre-school language difficulties go on to develop dyslexia. It has been found that auditory working memory difficulties and phonological processing problems are frequently observed not only in dyslexic children but also in children who have a language difficulty – which makes them good candidates for being shared cognitive difficulties in these two disorders. There may well be non-shared cognitive difficulties also, in that for instance we might expect to see grammar and vocabulary difficulties in children who have a language disorder but not necessarily in dyslexic children. Some studies have suggested that auditory processing difficulties are quite often seen in children with language disorders but they are not usually present in dyslexic children. (Auditory processing difficulties are evident when a child is found to have trouble in processing not only speech sounds but also other sorts of sounds, like for instance tones or musical sounds.) Figure 5.1 shows the Venn diagram for dyslexia and co-occurring DLD.

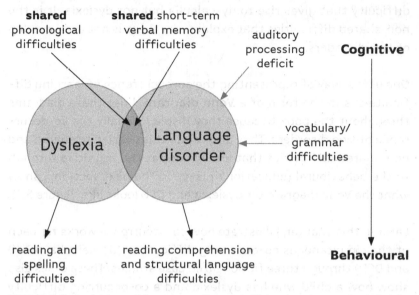

Figure 5.1: Dyslexia and language disorder: Shared and non-shared risks

The partial overlap of the Venn circles reflects the co-occurrence of dyslexia and language disorder. At the cognitive level (upper part of the Venn diagram), we can see that short-term auditory memory and phonological awareness difficulties contribute to both disorders; these are the shared cognitive difficulties. In contrast vocabulary/grammar difficulties and auditory processing deficits contribute only to language disorders, and are, therefore, the non-shared difficulties. The two disorders are expressed differently at the behavioural level (at the bottom of the Venn diagram), with dyslexia resulting in word-level reading and spelling difficulties while language disorder is expressed as oral language and (very likely also) reading comprehension difficulties.

LET'S RECAP

- Dyslexic children often have at least one co-occurring (or accompanying) learning difficulty, for example maths, attention or motor difficulties.
- The co-occurrence (or overlap) of two learning disorders is explained by their having a shared learning difficulty;

for instance, an auditory working memory deficit being shared across dyslexia and language disorder.
- Non-shared learning difficulties are specific to a particular disorder and explain the lack of a total overlap of two disorders; for instance, auditory processing difficulties are seen in many children with language difficulties but not in children with dyslexia.

Dyslexia and co-occurring arithmetic (maths) difficulties/dyscalculia

The at-risk study I described earlier shows that dyslexia commonly co-occurs with arithmetic/maths difficulties, and that for many poor readers their maths weaknesses may be as severe as their difficulties with literacy. What do we expect to see in children with specific arithmetic difficulties that are also called dyscalculia?

- Children with dyscalculia have difficulties with number facts and calculation. For instance:
  - they have a poor understanding of numbers, their relative size and their relationships with each other (e.g. understanding that six is bigger than three)
  - they count on their fingers instead of remembering their 'number bonds'
  - they get 'lost' in the middle of carrying out a calculation
  - some children also have difficulties with mathematical reasoning (e.g. using maths concepts, facts or computations to solve word problems).
- The child's arithmetic skills are well below those expected for their age and they significantly affect how they cope in maths lessons at school.
- The arithmetic difficulties are obvious throughout the school years, though for some children with milder problems their weaknesses may not be evident until maths demands on the them increase, usually at

secondary school and especially when they have to work under speed conditions (as in timed tests).

A brief summary of arithmetic disorder/dyscalculia and its causes is given in Box 5.1.

Box 5.1: Specific arithmetic disorder or dyscalculia

Specific arithmetic disorder or dyscalculia are diagnostic labels used to describe children who find it very difficult to acquire maths concepts and to calculate with numbers accurately. Arithmetic difficulties affect around 6 per cent of our child population and they commonly co-occur with reading difficulties.

There is good agreement that many children who find arithmetic difficult have a basic deficit in **numerosity**. Numerosity (also sometimes called number sense) describes a difficulty in appreciating the magnitude of number (i.e. understanding number size or quantity). To give you a better understanding of what numerosity is, it is helpful to look at tasks that measure numerosity. These include:

- counting a set of dots accurately (e.g. 'How many dots are in this box?')
- deciding which of two written numbers is the bigger (digit comparison) (e.g. 'Which is the bigger number, 2 or 3?')
- deciding which of two boxes contains the more dots (dot comparison) (e.g. 'Which of these two boxes has more dots?').

Children with specific arithmetic difficulties perform these tasks less accurately and more slowly than children who have no arithmetic difficulties. Tests of numerosity have also been demonstrated to be good longitudinal predictors of later arithmetic ability – that is, struggling to do 'count the dots' or dot-and digit comparisons at a young age predicts poor maths performance later on.

There are, however, other cognitive deficits that might be expected to contribute to the development of arithmetic difficulties. A different possible cognitive cause is having a visual–spatial difficulty; tasks that measure visual–spatial ability would be copying patterns with blocks and doing jig-saw puzzles. A visual–spatial difficulty can affect visually based mathematical concepts like understanding geometry and symmetry, interpreting graphs and visual diagrams, cal-culating measurement and understanding the visual basis of fractions.

Around 20–30 per cent of children who have dyslexia are also likely to have arithmetic difficulties, indicating a high degree of overlap between reading and arithmetic disorders. Studies have shown that children who have both disorders have problems of both phonological awareness and numerosity. These children have difficulty analysing sounds in words, which affects their read-ing and spelling, and they also struggle with numerosity, which leads to their arithmetic difficulties. In contrast, children with only reading (but not arithmetic) difficulties have no trouble with numerosity, and children with only arithmetic (but not reading) difficulties have no trouble with phonological awareness. We can conclude, therefore, that phonological and numerosity deficits are the non-shared cognitive features in these two disorders. And in some children, weaknesses in visual spatial abilities that impact the grasp of visual concepts in maths could be expected to func-tion as a non-shared risk specific to dyscalculia.

The next question we can ask is: what is the shared cognitive difficulty which explains the overlap of dyslexia and dyscalculia? It seems that arithmetic skill is related to early verbal number skills (in particular learning the number labels and being able to count); these skills in turn are influenced by even earlier oral lan-guage skills. Thus, early language difficulties may explain the co-occurrence of literacy and arithmetic disorders. Auditory working memory may be of particular importance. Children with arithmetic difficulties cannot easily 'hold on to' numbers in their working memory while they add or subtract them.

LET'S RECAP

- The shared cognitive difficulty in dyslexia and dyscalculia (specific arithmetic disorder) is most probably a language difficulty, which would include auditory working memory weaknesses.
- The non-shared cognitive difficulties are presumed to be phonological weakness that is specific to dyslexia, while numerosity deficits and visual spatial difficulties are specific to dyscalculia/arithmetic disorder.

A proposed Venn diagram for dyslexia and dyscalculia is shown in Figure 5.2.

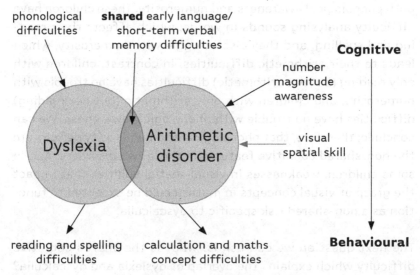

Figure 5.2: Dyslexia and arithmetic disorder: Shared and non-shared risks

CASE STUDY 2: JYOTI, A CHILD WITH DYSLEXIA AND DYSCALCULIA

Jyoti, aged nine years, was referred for assessment by her parents, with the support of her teachers at an independent day school where she is currently in Year 4. Her parents are concerned about her difficulties in understanding concepts in maths, her slow speed of working, her difficulties in transferring her thoughts to paper, her struggles with spatial materials and her weaknesses in spelling. A report from her  class teachers described her as being currently average in her class in reading, but having made slow progress in Reception and Year 1. She is, however, performing below class standards in spelling, written work and maths. There are no teacher concerns about her overall concentration, though Jyoti has been observed to have difficulty in following instructions, processing information and planning strategies (especially in maths). Jyoti is described as a motivated, enthusiastic, co-operative and hard-working girl who gets on well with her teachers and her classmates. She attends weekly spelling support groups and she has access to in-class support for maths. The school's SENCo has been working on her spelling, spatial abilities and maths. In addition to the learning support Jyoti has received at school, she had an outside school tutor in Years 1–3. In Year 4, she started at an external tutoring centre, which provided a report indicating that Jyoti has been working on maths, including her speed of calculating numbers, through worksheet practice.

Jyoti's pre-school speech and language development was a little delayed. Her family is second generation Indian, though Jyoti has had exposure only to English as both her mother tongue and language of education. Jyoti had an assessment by a speech and language therapist when she was aged five years. It was found that she had good listening attention and social interaction skills and there were no concerns about her understanding of language though her expressive language skills were a little underdeveloped. Some specific speech sound difficulties were observed and it was noted that her phonological awareness was delayed. Jyoti went on to receive some speech and language therapy sessions over the course of the next year, which particularly focused on improving her pronunciation and developing better phonological awareness. There is a family history of reading and spelling difficulties (father).

We will take up Jyoti's story again in Chapter 7 (assessment) and Chapter 10 (intervention).

Dyslexia and co-occurring attention difficulties/ADHD

Many parents and teachers complain that children with literacy difficulties seem to find it hard to concentrate. This raises the issue of whether these children might also have co-occurring ADHD. The problem here is that it can be hard for psychologists such as myself (and of course parents and teachers too) to disentangle whether we are looking at a true attention difficulty (such as ADHD) or whether we might be seeing a secondary behavioural consequence (or side-effect) of the literacy disorder. Many children with reading difficulties become frustrated by their failure to learn to read and this can lead to deteriorating motivation and increasing disengagement, especially as they get older. In the classroom, such a child might be seen as distracted, 'daydreamy' and generally 'switched off'. It is these behaviours that parents and teachers might be tempted to describe as an attention difficulty, but in some children these may be more appropriately described as an understandable behavioural reaction to having a learning difficulty.

This is nicely demonstrated in a recent research study that followed a large number of children through childhood and adolescence, and identified a small number of individuals who appeared to have 'late onset ADHD' (i.e. children who showed no signs of ADHD in early childhood but who were doing so by mid-adolescence) (Cooper *et al.*, 2018). Interestingly, these children had shown low scores on reading and spelling tests when they were seen at age nine. Children with reading/spelling difficulties might not exhibit ADHD-like behaviours at primary school, but as they move into secondary school they are placed under increased academic pressure; this in turn can set the scene for developing problems of motivation and disengagement, which might be mistakenly labelled as ADHD.

It is also important to bear in mind that ADHD can look very different in girls than boys. Research has shown that girls are more likely to present as inattentive, 'daydreamy' and withdrawn, whereas boys often show high levels of overactivity and behaviour problems (as well as attention difficulties). This means that boys are more often diagnosed with ADHD because they create a greater problem for parents and teachers.

Children with (true) ADHD present with two types of difficulty:

1. They are **inattentive**, which shows as wandering off task, lacking persistence (giving up easily), having difficulty keeping focused and being easily distracted.
2. They are hyperactive and impulsive (boys especially). **Hyperactivity** means that the child moves around a lot when it is not appropriate, or it may take the form of being very fidgety, tapping their fingers or shaking their foot all the time, or talking too much. **Impulsivity** means hasty actions that occur in the moment without thinking ahead and that may even cause harm to the child, such as darting into the road without looking.

Being inattentive, overactive and impulsive interferes with the child's day-to-day life and can affect learning within the classroom.

Around 5 per cent of the child population has ADHD; it tends to be persisting and it is thought to be more common in boys than girls (although as we saw earlier, girls can be under-diagnosed because they present rather differently from boys). Behaviour problems are frequently seen alongside ADHD, in particular, oppositional defiant disorder (ODD); these are children who 'don't do what they're told' – nearly all the time!

A brief summary of the features of ADHD, including its causes, is given in Box 5.2.

Box 5.2: Attention deficit hyperactivity disorder (ADHD)

ADHD is a disorder of attention that affects children's learning and behaviour in a wide range of settings, not just the classroom but also the broader environment – at home and when out with friends. Because many children with ADHD respond well to prescription medication (e.g. Ritalin), it has been suggested that ADHD is caused by a chemical imbalance in the brain.

What is the cognitive explanation for ADHD? One theory is that it is caused by **executive dysfunction**. Executive abilities are skills that are required to get tasks done, be organized, control impulses and be adaptable and resilient; these are important to many of the demands of everyday life and of school. There are thought to be a number of skills that are part of executive function and that include being able to:

- sustain attention
- inhibit responses when needed
- control emotions
- get started on tasks
- plan and organize
- manage time
- set goals
- be persistent but also flexible.

Another theory is that children with ADHD have what we call **delay aversion**, which explains why they are almost always impulsive and reward seeking. Many children with ADHD would prefer to have an instant reward rather than a larger reward given after a delay. For instance, if told that they can eat one sweet immediately or if they are able to wait five minutes they can eat two sweets, children with ADHD would rather eat one sweet immediately whereas typically developing children are more likely to be able to 'hold back' and so get the extra sweet.

The co-occurrence rate of dyslexia and ADHD is between 25 and 40 per cent.

The non-shared difficulties in these co-occurring disorders are phonological processing weaknesses, which are specific to dyslexia, and executive dysfunction, which is specific to ADHD. An executive difficulty that is thought to be of particular importance in ADHD is **response disinhibition**. This means that children with ADHD find it very hard to 'hold back' or stop themselves doing what they shouldn't. It is the response disinhibition in the child with ADHD that explains why their parents and teachers often say, 'He doesn't think before he acts', which results in quite a lot of accidents, mistakes and, of course, behaviour problems.

And what is the shared difficulty that explains the overlap of literacy disorders with ADHD? Research has shown us that this is likely to be slow processing speed. Children with literacy difficulties are slow to process print and sounds, while children with ADHD have been found to be slow and error prone when processing information generally.

LET'S RECAP

- Dyslexia and ADHD commonly co-occur.
- The shared difficulty explaining the overlap of these disorders is slow processing speed.
- The non-shared difficulties are phonological processing weaknesses specific to dyslexia, and trouble with inhibiting behaviour, which is specific to children with ADHD.

The Venn diagram describing the shared and non-shared deficits in dyslexia and ADHD is given in Figure 5.3.

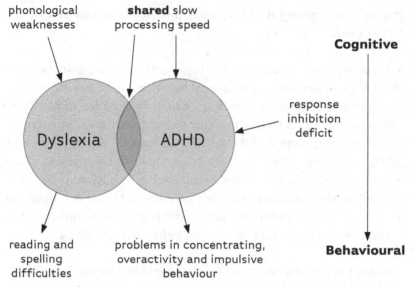

Figure 5.3: Dyslexia and ADHD: Shared and non-shared risks

CASE STUDY 3: BILLY, WHO HAS DYSLEXIA AND ADHD

Billy, aged seven years, was referred for assessment by his parents and teachers who want to have a better understanding of his abilities, his educational attainments and his difficulties with concentration. Billy attends a state school where he appeared to do well in the Nursery and Reception classes, apart from some concerns about his high activity level and his difficulties focusing. However, by the end of Year 1, he was finding written work increasingly difficult and he was becoming somewhat distracted and tired. In Year 2, he was struggling with writing and his progress in spelling was poor. These problems continued through Year 2 and now on into Year 3. Billy was not a late reader and in fact he loves books and he reads accurately and with good understanding. His parents have, however, noted that he will sometimes guess at unfamiliar words and he is not confident with phonics. A helpful report from his school described him as achieving averagely in his class in reading and maths, but below class expectation in spelling and written work. He is slow to produce written work and finds it hard to remember spelling patterns and rules. He is not as yet receiving any extra help. Billy's teachers commented on his having poor focus and he tires quickly; he is also easily distracted in class. He finds it hard to remember more than one instruction at a time. Nonetheless, his teachers recognize that he is a bright and articulate little boy. Billy's parents commented that his confidence had declined over the course of the last year or so, and at times he is reluctant to do his homework. Although a generally generous and thoughtful child, he can show occasional stubborn and oppositional behaviour.

Billy's early speech and language development were good. He is a generally healthy little boy. There is a family history of dyslexia on both sides (his father's mother and three of his father's cousins, together with a cousin on his mother's side who has both dyslexia and dyspraxia).

We will return to Billy's story later, in the chapters that cover assessment and intervention.

Dyslexia and co-occurring motor difficulties

Many children with dyslexia seem to have handwriting difficulties too – and their written work is often messy and disorganized. This raises the issue of such children having not only dyslexia but also a separate co-occurring disorder that affects their handwriting. When children's handwriting and organization struggles are due to difficulties with visual motor skills and motor organization, they may be described as having developmental coordination disorder (DCD), sometimes called dyspraxia in the UK.

There are three main features of DCD:

1. The child's motor skills are well below those to be expected given their chronological age; they are often clumsy and they have problems controlling their arms, legs, hands and fingers.

2. Their motor difficulties interfere with daily living activities such as self-care (e.g. dressing themselves, using a knife and fork), as well as affecting their writing skills at school.

3. Their difficulties are not due to poor vision, general slow learning or a neurological condition such as cerebral palsy.

Around 5–6 per cent of primary-age children have DCD, with boys being more likely to be affected than girls. Delayed motor milestones (e.g. being late to learn to walk) are usually the first sign of DCD in pre-schoolers. In the middle years, there are difficulties with handwriting, ball games and organization. Most children with DCD have motor problems that persist well into their secondary school years. DCD very commonly co-occurs with ADHD and perhaps a little less often with literacy disorders.

A brief summary of the features of DCD and its hypothesized cognitive basis is given in Box 5.3.

Box 5.3: Developmental coordination disorder (DCD)

DCD most obviously shows as difficulties with motor function, including handwriting, handling tools and implements and so on. However, it is important to realize that virtually all the movements we make are heavily dependent on perceptual input, particularly the information we get from vision, but also from our vestibular (balance) system and through proprioception (our sense of body movement). For this reason, it may be better to think of movement skills as perceptual motor skills rather than simply motor skills. Some children with DCD show particular difficulties with fine motor skills (hand movement related), which would be expected to affect their handwriting. Others show mostly difficulties with gross motor skills (involving whole body movements), which means that we would expect them to be clumsy and to do badly at sport.

Children with DCD are thought to have difficulty in relating positions of objects they see in their visual space to positions they experience in their motor space – in other words, they find it hard to relate 'seen' positions to 'felt' positions. They find it hard to process size, length and shape information when they are presented with a visual task and this then leads to difficulty in producing movements that are guided accurately in space – whether these are fine or gross movements.

Dyslexia and DCD frequently co-occur; it has been estimated that as many as 40 per cent of children with dyslexia also have motor difficulties that affect their drawing ability, their handwriting and their ability to play sport.

Why do dyslexia and DCD co-occur? It seems obvious that the non-shared deficits in co-occurring dyslexia and DCD are a phonological deficit explaining the dyslexia and a visual/spatial/perceptual deficit explaining the DCD. Finding a shared deficit that explains the overlap of the two disorders has proved more challenging. We know that processing speed deficits are seen across a wide range of learning difficulties; because of this, we sometimes talk about processing speed difficulties being a **domain general deficit**. So we see slow processing in children with dyslexia, DLD, dyscalculia, ADHD and DCD. It could be, therefore, that slow processing speed is the shared feature in dyslexia and DCD, though as yet we have no direct evidence for this.

The features explaining the co-occurrence of dyslexia and DCD are shown in the Venn diagram in Figure 5.4.

LET'S RECAP

- Dyslexia and developmental coordination disorder (DCD) commonly co-occur, which explains why we see quite a lot of children with literacy difficulties who also have problems with handwriting.
- The non-shared deficit specific to DCD is a perceptual

motor difficulty, which results in poor handwriting, while the non-shared deficit in dyslexia is of course a phonological weakness.

- Finding a shared deficit that explains why dyslexia and DCD co-occur has proved challenging, but slow processing speed is a possible candidate.

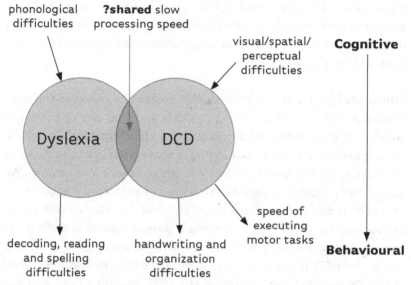

Figure 5.4: Dyslexia and DCD: Shared and non-shared risks

● CASE STUDY 4: FREDDIE, WHO HAS DYSLEXIA AND DCD/DYSPRAXIA

Freddie, aged 12 years, was referred for assessment by his parents, on the advice and recommendation of Ms B, his special needs and English teacher, at a state comprehensive school where he is now in Year 8. His parents and teachers first became aware of his difficulties with reading and writing (both spelling and handwriting) by the end of Reception. He continued to struggle in Years 1 and 2 but was able to pass his Key Stage 1 Standard Assessment Tests (SATs). He very much 'bumped along' the bottom of his class in Years 3–5, so his parents set up outside-school phonics tuition for him. His Year 6 teacher was very concerned about his slow progress and arranged for him to have one-to-one literacy tuition on a regular weekly basis. He was also allowed extra time when sitting his Key Stage 2 SATs. He passed his English and maths but failed the SPAG (spelling and grammar) aspect of the assessment.

Freddie moved to secondary school and by half-way through his first year his English teacher had identified him as a student needing extra support. He attended a special reading pro-gramme after it was found that he scored at a very low level on a reading test. He made a lot of progress and his teachers now view him as reading at a much higher level. Freddie seems to be finding maths easier than literacy and he is in the middle set in maths. He is not currently receiving any additional learning support, although a helpful report from his teachers acknowl-edged his continuing difficulties with spelling, handwriting and written work. This has caused Freddie increasing frustration over the years, which means he sometimes becomes disengaged and 'switched off' at school. His frustration occasionally spills over into anger outbursts at home. Freddie's parents and Ms B felt it important to have a better understanding of the nature and extent of his written output difficulties, hence the current referral.

Freddie was ahead of his age with his early milestones for walk-ing, talking and so on. He did, however, find drawing difficult during his pre-school and early primary years. There are no health problems. There is a family history of spelling difficulties (Freddie's mother).

KEY MESSAGES TO TAKE AWAY

✓ As many as 40 per cent of children with one learning difficulty will also have another separate learning difficulty; this indicates a high rate of co-occurrence.
✓ It is suggested that 'shared' causes (at both the genetic and

cognitive levels) explain why learning difficulties co-occur or overlap with each other; however, there are also 'non-shared' causes that appear to be specific to a given learning difficulty.

✓ In dyslexia co-occurring with developmental language disorder (DLD), auditory working memory and phonological awareness weaknesses are shared difficulties, while vocabulary/grammar and auditory processing deficits specific to language disorder are likely non-shared difficulties.

✓ In dyslexia co-occurring with arithmetic disorders/dyscalculia, it is thought that the shared cognitive difficulty is early language (including auditory working memory) difficulties; the non-shared difficulties are phonological deficits that are specific to dyslexia, while numerosity and visual spatial weaknesses are specific to dyscalculia.

✓ In dyslexia co-occurring with ADHD, it has been shown that the most likely shared difficulty across these two disorders is slow processing speed, while the non-shared difficulties are phonological awareness, which is unique to reading ability, and response disinhibition, which is unique to ADHD.

✓ In dyslexia co-occurring with DCD, the non-shared difficulties are a phonological deficit explaining the dyslexia and a visual/spatial/perceptual deficit explaining the DCD, while a possible shared deficit is slow processing speed.

PART 2

HOW TO SUPPORT AND HELP

Chapter 6

How We Identify and Assess Literacy Difficulties

In this chapter I describe how:

→ class teachers can look out for signs that would indicate that a child in their class might have a literacy difficulty
→ teachers can share their concerns with the child's parents to create a working partnership
→ screening for literacy difficulties might be done in schools so that children are identified as early as possible
→ Individual Educational Plans (IEPs) are used to target a child's difficulties, describe what special teaching should be set in place for them and aid communication between professionals and parents
→ a comprehensive assessment not only 'diagnoses' a child's literacy difficulty, but also indicates patterns of learning strength and weakness that direct us to the teaching methods that best meet their individual needs
→ teachers can get the most out of the assessor's oral feedback and written report, drawing on our case study of Alex (who has dyslexia and language difficulties) as an illustrative example.

Now that you have the knowledge about literacy difficulties that was covered in Part 1 of the book, we can at last turn our attention to the practical aspects of identifying, assessing and supporting the child with a literacy problem. Recall from Part 1 that there are signs that are evident even before a child starts school: lateness in talking, muddling speech sounds and being born into a family of poor readers and spellers. As a teacher, you will not necessarily know which of your pupils is more likely to have a literacy difficulty on the basis of their early speech and language development or their family history, but this is information you can obtain through talking to parents and looking at nursery school records and reports. If you see a pupil struggling during the first two years at school you will want to 'catch the problem before it worsens'. If a pupil seems to get off to a reasonable start in reading but progress slows by say Year 4, you might ask, 'Does this child have a difficulty not so much with reading but with spelling and getting their ideas down on paper – could this be mild dyslexia?'

Screening for literacy problems (dyslexia in particular) is currently very topical and I will look at how that could be done. Once a child has been identified as having a literacy difficulty, it is important to ensure that extra help is put in place so that they can make better progress – and that progress needs to be monitored. Children who continue to make slow progress will likely need a more detailed assessment of their learning problems, and I describe what such an assessment should look like and what you and the child's parents should expect to get from it. We conclude by following up Alex (introduced in Chapter 4) as an example of identifying and assessing a literacy difficulty in a child who has experienced early speech and language delay.

Could a pupil in my class have a literacy difficulty and what do I do about it?

★ Checklist (downloadable from www.jkp.com/ catalogue/book/9781839977046)

Could the child have dyslexia? Five key questions you can ask (tick YES or NO as appropriate); some of these questions will need to be answered by the child's parents with some additional information from nursery school records.

	YES	NO
If you are a Reception class teacher:		
1. Is the child proving to be later than their classmates in starting to learn to read?	☐	☐
2. Are they struggling to learn the letters of the alphabet?	☐	☐
3. Was the child late in learning to talk or was their speech unclear as a pre-schooler?	☐	☐
4. Do they find it hard to play 'sound games' like 'I Spy'?	☐	☐
5. Have members of the child's family had difficulties with reading and spelling?	☐	☐
If you are a Year 1 or 2 teacher:		
1. Is the child struggling with reading and are they behind other children in their class?	☐	☐
2. Do they find spelling hard and make mistakes, even on simple words?	☐	☐
3. Are they reluctant to read in class?	☐	☐
4. Do they find it hard to decode words they have not seen before?	☐	☐
5. Have members of the child's family had difficulties with reading and spelling?	☐	☐

	YES	NO
If you are a Year 3–6 teacher:		
1. Did the child seem to be 'okay' with reading early on in primary school but is now falling behind?	☐	☐
2. Do they read slowly?	☐	☐
3. Do they struggle with spelling and find it hard to remember words from their spelling lists?	☐	☐
4. Are they reluctant to read and write – so they actively 'avoid reading and writing'?	☐	☐
5. Have members of the child's family had difficulties with reading and spelling?	☐	☐

If you have answered yes to at least three of the five questions in the relevant section, your pupil may be showing signs of dyslexia.

Could the child have a reading comprehension difficulty? Here are key questions to ask; again some of these questions will need to be answered by the child's parents with some additional information from nursery school records and earlier primary school reports.

	YES	NO
If you are an early years primary school teacher:		
1. Did the child pick up reading quite quickly but has now lost interest in books?	☐	☐
2. Do they find it hard to understand and remember what they have read?	☐	☐
3. Do they find it difficult to follow the plot of a story or presentation?	☐	☐
4. Do they find it hard to follow and remember a list of instructions?	☐	☐

	YES	NO
5. Do they seem to have quite a limited vocabulary and to struggle to express themselves orally?	☐	☐
6. Were they late to talk as a pre-schooler?	☐	☐

If you are a later years primary or secondary school teacher:

	YES	NO
1. Does the child read out loud well but find it hard to understand and remember what they have read?	☐	☐
2. Do they avoid reading?	☐	☐
3. Do they find it hard to follow a conversation or the story line of a film/TV show, or to remember a list of instructions?	☐	☐
4. Do they seem to have quite a limited vocabulary?	☐	☐
5. Were they a late talker?	☐	☐

If you have answered yes to at least three of these questions in the relevant section, your pupil may be showing signs of a reading comprehension difficulty which, if you recall from Part 1, is strongly associated with underlying language difficulties.

What you should do about it

Step 1: Approach your pupil's parent or carer and discuss your concerns with them. You might arrange a special appointment or perhaps wait for the next routine parent–teacher meeting to do this. It is important from the outset to work towards a good partnership with the child's parent/s. Involving parents is critical to ensuring the child progresses well, as parents play an important role in supporting and motivating their child as well as reinforcing their learning at home. The best approach is to let the child's parents know what you as a teacher are concerned about, while also listening to their views. It is worth writing down a list of your observations and concerns, using your answers to the questions you've asked yourself from the previous section of this chapter. Do ask the parents about not only their own views of their child's progress in reading and writing, but also their pre-school history (in particular, their early speech and language development) and whether other members of their family have had reading and spelling difficulties. This then enables you to put together your shared observations in the broader context of the child's development.

Of course, some parents will be more receptive to your concerns than others. You may need to tread carefully here and judge the right moment to approach a reluctant parent, and then after you've described your concerns, perhaps give them a little time to take on board what you've said. In the meantime, gather more evidence (perhaps even bring together examples of areas where the child is struggling) and then arrange a further meeting with the parents. Keep in mind that if you feel a 'bit stuck' in getting a dialogue going with the child's parents, you could always approach the SENCo or the deputy or headteacher to see if they could become involved in moving matters forward.

Of course, there is the opposite extreme where you as a teacher are satisfied that a pupil is progressing well in literacy but their parents see them as having a problem. You will need to ask them what observations they have made that have generated their concerns (and again check on developmental and family history which may be a source of their worries). Share with the parents your own observations and if possible give concrete evidence of their child's reading and writing levels – by telling them what level books the child is reading, showing them samples of their writing and so on. If they remain unconvinced, ask the SENCo to perhaps carry out some simple tests or use checklists that should provide objective evidence of the child's level of literacy skills. If the child's levels are well up to class expectation, the parents should feel reassured that all is well, but it is worth adding that you will keep an eye on their future progress.

Step 2: Work together on a plan of action. Could it be that the child needs a little more time? In which case, it is a question of keeping an eye on their progress over the next term to see how they get on and whether their progress improves or not. Perhaps involve the class's teaching assistant (if there is one) in providing extra reading and writing practice. Encourage the child's parents to listen to them read for ten minutes a day and perhaps offer some tips for learning weekly spelling lists and so on. Check on progress after a term or so. If there has been good progress, then you and your pupil's parents will feel reassured that all is on track. If not, then it will be important to take the next step.

Step 3: Involve the school's SENCo. The SENCo will want to talk through your concerns about the child and may suggest that they be placed on the school's Special Needs Register. This means that they will not only continue to 'be kept an eye on', but their progress will be monitored and extra help provided. An Individual Educational Plan will be set up for them (see below) and they may well be able to receive additional support and teaching. The extra help could take the form of a classroom assistant paying the child more attention and supporting them in the classroom or they might be included in 'catch up' groups. The SENCo may want to carry out some tests of the child's learning and their literacy skills in order to get a better idea of what they know (and don't know) and where their underlying difficulties lie. These tests might include asking them to read lists of real words and nonsense words, getting them to do phonological awareness games, having them read a story out loud and then answer questions on what it was about, and so on. If the child continues to make slow progress after say 6–12 months, it could be that the SENCo recommends you move on to the next step.

Step 4: Carry out a more detailed assessment of their learning and their literacy difficulties. This could be carried out by a specialist teacher, visiting educational psychologist or an independent (clinical or educational) psychologist. Getting such an assessment in these difficult times when resources are both limited and costly can be a challenge. Some parents may want to arrange and to pay for an assessment themselves. If they do decide to pursue this course of action, you may be in a position to recommend a specialist teacher or psychologist that you and your colleagues have worked with in the past. If that isn't a possibility, you could suggest that they find a qualified teacher assessor through an organization like PATOSS (Professional Association of Teachers of Students with Specific Learning Difficulties) or a clinical or educational psychologist listed on the British Psychological Society's website (note that psychologists should be registered with the Health and Care Professions Council).

Should we routinely screen for literacy difficulties?

There has been a lot of interest of late in screening young children for literacy difficulties so that they are identified at as young an age as possible before they fall too far behind – and become more frustrated and 'turned off' reading. If we can pick up poor readers early on in primary school and give them additional support and the right kind of help, we can ensure that they leave primary school with the literacy skills and the self-confidence and motivation to cope with the demands of a secondary school curriculum. Box 6.1 outlines what teachers might do to set up an effective screening programme in the early school years.

> **Box 6.1**: How to screen young
> children for literacy difficulties
> Two common features in children who go on to develop
> reading difficulties are a **family history** (being born into a
> family where a close family member, usually a parent, has
> had reading and spelling problems) and **slow (or disordered)
> early speech and language development**. Information
> about these features can be sought from parents and/or
> nursery school records; it provides a good starting point for
> monitoring closely these children's early response to reading
> instruction.
>
> It is, of course, important for teachers to draw on their own
> observations and knowledge of the child's reading skills and
> progress within the classroom. Skills related to reading that
> you as a teacher can readily observe and rate might include:
>
> - the quality of the child's oral language, in particular
>   the size of their vocabulary and their ability to
>   express themselves in full sentences

- how easily they learn the alphabet letters, both identifying and writing them
- their ability to recognize and analyse sounds in spoken words (phonological awareness)
- how easily they build up a basic sight word reading vocabulary.

You can draw on existing instruments (Reception Baseline Assessment, Early Years Foundation Stage Profile, Year 1 Phonics Screening Check) which provide additional reliable information. Results of Key Stage SATs might also be used if available. Commercially produced early language and literacy screening tests are now being used in many schools, for instance NELI (Nuffield Early Language Intervention Screener).

Verbally able children who go on to display literacy difficulties later in primary schooling may not be so readily 'picked up' by early screening measures. These children's difficulties could be detected through tests of phonic decoding (non-word reading) and of spelling in a second round of screening conducted in Years 4, 5 or 6.

Children identified as poor readers following screening require intervention (i.e. specialist teaching using evidence-based programmes) and their response to intervention should be closely monitored.

The Individual Educational Plan

Children on the Special Needs Register will usually have an Individual Educational Plan (IEP) which summarizes the child's difficulties and sets out what they will need to support their learning difficulties at school. It not only states clearly how the child's special needs will be met, but it is also a good way to aid communication between SENCo, classroom teachers and parents. IEPs may be constructed a little differently from school to school, but they should cover the same key elements. They should have:

- **targets** that the child needs to achieve
- **learning support strategies** that are put in place for the child to reach their targets
- **criteria** for successful achievement of the targets
- **a record** of the dates on which the criteria were met.

IEPs are generally reviewed termly so that the child's progress can be formally monitored and tracked. Towards the end of this chapter, we will look at one of Alex's IEPs.

LET'S RECAP

- If, as a teacher, you suspect a pupil has a literacy difficulty, you need to ask questions that help you to identify specific concerns.
- Using standardized screening instruments can provide helpful supplementary information to back up your informal observations of the child's learning.
- You then need to share your observations with the child's parents and the SENCo in order work out a plan of action that might include monitoring the child's progress, and if needed, setting in place extra support.
- If progress is slow, the SENCo may consider pursuing a more detailed assessment of the child's difficulties as well as drawing up an Individual Educational Plan.

Assessing the child with a literacy difficulty

Formal assessments of children's literacy difficulties are carried out by specialist teachers or by psychologists. They usually involve asking the child to do standardized tests that compare their performance on a particular skill to that of a large group of same age children (the normative sample) – to see if the child achieves in line with their age group, above it or below. Of course, specialist teachers and psychologists don't just look at test scores. Importantly, they try to put the child's learning profile or pattern (based on the test scores) within the broader context of the child's developmental and schooling history. They take note also of the child's way of doing a task and the sort of mistakes they make. Test behaviour is important too − how co-operative and motivated the child is, how well they concentrate, what their self-esteem is like and so on.

Before the assessor sees the child, it is usual for them to obtain **detailed background information** from parents and teachers about their concerns, what they themselves have observed and the questions they are asking about the child's learning. As a teacher you might be asked, either face-to-face or in a questionnaire (and sometimes both), questions like:

- What are your concerns about the child's progress in literacy?
- Does the child seem to have additional problems such as struggling to concentrate, being clumsy, or having difficulties with maths?
- What extra help has the child already had and do you think it has made a difference?
- Does the child appear generally happy at school and do they get on well with you, their teacher, and with their classmates?
- Does the child have behaviour problems and if so, what form do they take?

You will also be asked to provide relevant information from school reports and results from standardized instruments such as the Phonics Screening Check or SATs results.

Tests that assessors use
TESTS OF INTELLIGENCE (IQ) OR GENERAL COGNITIVE ABILITY
The use of IQ tests in literacy assessments is sometimes viewed as unnecessary, partly because we know that literacy difficulties are seen in children of all abilities, but also because research has shown us that specific literacy difficulties are caused by underlying language processing weaknesses (not from having a low IQ). So why bother with an ability index like IQ at all? The reasons for giving IQ or ability tests are that, first, they can tell us a lot about a child's pattern of learning, including what they are strong at and what

they are weak at. Second, they can help us identify the type of learning difficulty a child has. Finally, they can guide parents and teachers towards having the right level of expectation for a child.

Let's unpick this a little by explaining what an IQ test, like the well-known Wechsler Intelligence Scale for Children (WISC) (Wechsler, 2014, 2016, 2017), consists of. This is a test commonly used by educational and clinical psychologists. The WISC does not just come up with a single overall IQ figure that reflects how generally able a child is; it does more than that. In fact, it consists of five scales of ability which make it possible to look at different components or aspects of the child's learning:

- **Verbal Comprehension Scale** – this consists of orally administered tests of verbal reasoning and of vocabulary knowledge.
- **Visual Spatial Scale** – this non-verbal scale makes use of coloured blocks and puzzles that look at the child's visual perception and spatial ability.
- **Processing Speed Scale** – this consists of timed pencil-and-paper tests that assess visual motor and visual processing speeds.
- **Working Memory Scale** – these tests assess verbal and visual working memory.
- **Fluid Reasoning Scale** – this is another non-verbal scale that assesses visual perceptual and quantitative reasoning.

The child's performance on each subtest is expressed as a **scaled score** which has a mean (or average) of 10. So if a child scores around the 10 mark on Digit Span from the Working Memory Scale, for instance, it means that they have an average auditory working memory. A scaled score of well above 10 means that their working memory is strong and above average, while a scaled score that is well below 10 would indicate working memory difficulties. The child's performance on each scale is expressed as an **index score** which has a mean of 100. So if a child obtains a Verbal Comprehension Index score of around 100, it means that their oral language skills are average for their age. A high Verbal Comprehension Index score, say around the 120 mark, means that the child is highly verbally able, while a Verbal Comprehension Index score of 80 or below would be strongly suggestive of the child having oral language difficulties. It is possible to calculate a full-scale IQ, which is a composite figure based on several scores drawn from across all five scales. This provides an overall ability level and is again expressed as an index score with an average of 100.

The child who obtains a low score on the Verbal Comprehension Scale could well have language difficulties which will affect their classroom learning and their reading comprehension. Children who have relatively high scores on the Verbal Comprehension Scale but who struggle with the two non-verbal scales and the pencil-and paper tests from the Processing Speed Scale could have a developmental coordination disorder/dyspraxia. Children who have language and literacy difficulties often have a weak auditory working memory, which could be detected as a low score on the Digit Span subtest of the Working Memory Scale. Processing speed difficulties are seen across a wide range of specific learning difficulties so a low score on this scale is often seen in children who have literacy, language, visual motor, maths and attention difficulties.

What if a child scores low on all of the scales, indeed registers a below average full-scale IQ? These children struggle with all aspects of learning and could be described as having **generalized learning difficulties**. What needs to be recognized here is that the child's pace of learning will be slower than that of their classmates. As a result, parent and teacher expectations of the child's progress need to be kept modest; they often need a curriculum that is different from the other children in their class and which reflects the stage they are at in their learning; and they need lots of opportunities for practice and reinforcement of new concepts and skills.

There are some children who of course obtain well above average scores on all the indices, together with a high full-scale IQ. These children are very bright and it is appropriate for their parents and teachers to have high expectations for them at school. However, we sometimes see children who are very able (have a high IQ) but whose educational progress is slow. These children are experiencing

unexpected failure because their high IQ and index scores lead us to predict that they should be achieving well at school. For instance, the bright and articulate child who is unexpectedly struggling to learn to read could have dyslexia. And the bright child who is unexpectedly finding maths very difficult could have a specific arithmetic difficulty or dyscalculia.

TESTS OF EDUCATIONAL SKILLS

Here we are talking about attainment tests that cover skills that are taught in the classroom: reading, spelling, writing and maths. So that we can appreciate the different patterns that might be seen in a child with a literacy difficulty and to get the fullest possible picture of their performance at school, the assessor needs to test the following:

- **Single-word reading** – to assess the child's word reading vocabulary
- **Sentence or passage reading** – to see how well they read in context
- **Reading speed** – to assess how fast they read
- **Reading comprehension** – to see how well the child understands what they read
- **Non-word reading** – to assess phonic decoding ability
- **Spelling** – to assess ability to write single words spoken by the assessor
- **Writing** – to assess the child's handwriting legibility, their speed of writing and the quality of their written expression
- **Maths/Arithmetic** – to assess basic numerical operations, maths concepts and reasoning/problem solving.

Scores on tests of educational skills are usually given as standard scores (like the indices of an IQ test), with the mean or average being 100; scores around 100 indicate that the child is achieving at age expectation in the assessed skill, while scores significantly lower than 100 mean that they are achieving below expectation for their age, and scores substantially higher than 100 point to them achieving above age expectation.

TESTS OF SPECIFIC LEARNING DIFFICULTIES

These are sometimes called 'diagnostic' or 'marker' tests because they tap into the underlying learning deficits that are thought to cause the child's difficulty with literacy, maths and so on.

In the case of **dyslexia**, the tests that are diagnostically sensitive, and on which dyslexic children would be expected to perform badly, are:

- non-word reading, reflecting phonic decoding difficulties
- phonological awareness, which assess the child's ability to analyse the sounds in spoken words
- rapid naming (of letters, colours etc.), which tap into phonological processing skills
- phonological/auditory working memory such as Digit Span tests.

Tests that are sensitive to **developmental language disorder (DLD)**, which children with language difficulties would be expected to perform badly on, are:

- vocabulary and verbal reasoning
- auditory working memory
- non-word repetition, which assess auditory working memory and also aspects of articulation
- sentence repetition (repeating out loud lengthy sentences), which measure auditory memory, vocabulary knowledge and grammatical awareness
- listening comprehension of a passage that has been read to them.

There is now commercially available within the UK a set of diag-nostic language and literacy tests, the NELI Language and Literacy Screen, which is part of the Nuffield Early Language Intervention (NELI).[1] This is in the form of an iOS or Android app. The Language Screen assesses speaking and listening skills in children aged three-and-a-half through to nine years. There are four subtests

---

1   https://oxedandassessment.com/uk

that assess expressive vocabulary, receptive vocabulary, listening comprehension and sentence repetition, and together provide an overall language ability score. The NELI Language Screen has automatic scoring that generates a report and is designed for use by school staff, including classroom teachers and teaching assistants. It is aimed at identifying children in need of language intervention and is sensitive to language difficulties even in children for whom English is not their first language (see next section). What is very impressive is that the authors have demonstrated a very high correlation of 0.95 between the NELI Language Screen score and specialist language tests that are usually individually administered by speech and language therapists. NELI has also added a Reading Screen to its app packages.

Tests that are sensitive to developmental coordination disorder/ dyspraxia, specific arithmetic difficulty/dyscalculia and ADHD are described in the next chapter where we look at assessments of children who have these particular co-occurring disorders.

LET'S RECAP

- An assessment of the child with literacy difficulties typically begins with assessing their verbal and non-verbal abilities, their working memory and their processing speed – usually in the form of an IQ test.
- Attainment tests need to cover the full range of literacy skills, not just single-word reading but also prose reading, speed of reading, reading comprehension, spelling and writing skills (and arithmetic too).
- Diagnostic tests of dyslexia (and also sometimes of language) are needed to identify the underlying learning difficulties experienced by children who struggle with literacy.

What about testing children for whom English is not their first language?

The tests described earlier can be used for virtually all children presenting with a literacy difficulty and they cover a wide age range. However, there is one group of children who may present with literacy and language difficulties that provide an additional challenge for an assessor. These are children for whom English is not their first language, sometimes called **second language learners**. If a child who has been exposed to English only after entering school is struggling to read in their new language, could this be due to dyslexia? Or could it be due to their not having the oral language foundations that their English mother tongue classmates do? Box 6.2 provides some facts about language and literacy skills in children who do not have English as their first language.

Box 6.2: Facts about literacy and language in second language learners

- Most children from foreign language backgrounds have no difficulty in learning to read and spell in their second language of English.
- Because bilingual children have to learn the different sound systems of each of their languages, this draws their attention to the similarities and differences between them – which can make them more phonologically aware than their monolingual classmates (a definite advantage of bilingualism).
- If a bilingual child does not acquire word-level (accuracy) skills relatively quickly, this raises the possibility that they might have dyslexia; there is good evidence from research that tests of phonological awareness and letter knowledge are reliable in testing for dyslexia in bilingual children, even if they have been speaking English for only a short period of time.
- However, on the flip side, many bilingual children have long-term oral language difficulties (especially

---

in relation to their vocabulary knowledge), though this gap narrows a little over time; this has a 'knock-on' effect on educational skills, in particular reading comprehension, which is heavily dependent on having good oral language skills.

- We should never delay assessing bilingual children on the grounds of 'Don't worry, he'll catch up once his English is better'; if we do, it can mean that a dyslexic difficulty goes undetected or a child showing slow progress in oral English does not receive the support they need.

I will illustrate how second language learners are assessed in a case study (Susanna) in the next chapter.

How to read and understand the assessor's report

Once an assessment has taken place, it is usual for teachers and parents to be given the opportunity to discuss with the assessor what has been found out about the child's learning difficulties and how they can be helped. As well as receiving feedback about what the assessment showed, teachers and parents can ask questions to clarify their understanding of the child's difficulties and they can find out what can be done at school and at home to support them in their learning. The oral feedback is then followed by a written report. Listed below are the key areas that you can expect to see covered in the report:

- Why the referral was made in the first place.
- A description of the observations, views and concerns of parents and teachers.
- A summary of the test results (probably set out in a table).
- A description of the child's behaviour during testing.
- A statement of what the learning difficulty is – some assessors would describe this as a 'diagnosis' but others think that 'formulation' is a better, less medical-sounding term.

Very importantly, the report should have a detailed **recommendations** section which describes what can be done at school and at home to support the child so that their learning difficulties are well managed and their progress improved. The report should state:

- whether special teaching interventions are needed – how often these should be delivered, whether they should be conducted one-to-one or in a small group and who should deliver them
- what specialist teaching methods or programmes should be used to address the child's difficulties
- what parents can do at home to generally support their child and whether they should use specific strategies and teaching methods to aid and reinforce learning
- what parents and teachers can do to 'keep up' the child's motivation, self-esteem and confidence
- what accommodations can be made at school to support the child (extra time in exams, using a laptop instead of handwriting, having classroom notes printed out for them)
- what compensatory resources are available to the child that they can draw on to 'get round' their literacy difficulties (e.g. using their good vocabulary knowledge to correctly 'guess' at words in text, being highly motivated and hard working)
- whether a referral to another professional is needed to further explore the child's learning difficulties (e.g. a speech and language therapist or an occupational therapist)
- what might be expected to be done in the future and whether and when the child's progress should be reviewed.

Reports may also make some comments about **outcome**, which means predicting the child's likely future rate of progress and how this will look later on in their schooling. This is not an easy thing to do and its accuracy depends partly on how clear the child's learning profile is and, of course, on the knowledge and experience of the assessor. Making predictions about whether a child's outcome is likely to be positive or negative will be heavily influenced by the severity of the child's learning difficulty, together with the number of additional risks or co-occurring difficulties that are present. The able and articulate child with mild dyslexia and no co-occurring difficulties could potentially do very well at school and indeed go on to obtain high academic results and achieve considerable success in adult life. There are, of course, many examples of dyslexic individuals who have special talents and who have achieved great success in their chosen field, in spite of their struggles with reading and spelling – the celebrated architect Richard Rogers, the successful actress Jennifer Aniston, the famous entrepreneur Richard Branson and the celebrity chef Jamie Oliver. On the other hand, the child with severe dyslexia who also has co-occurring learning difficulties is far more likely to find academic study a challenge and may well leave school with few qualifications – and even experience low self-esteem that impacts their mental health.

It is important to bear in mind that for a given dyslexic child there are additional factors beyond their dyslexia that can influence whether they achieve well in school and are successful in adult life – or not! Non-dyslexia-related cognitive skills, additional risk factors and, very importantly, environmental experiences that impact outcome are sometimes referred to as **moderator variables**, which can be either positive or negative. These include early versus late identification, having a stimulating versus impoverished learning environment, high-quality intervention versus little or no intervention, having a low frustration tolerance and lack of resilience versus being motivated and resilient, and good versus poor parental support.

The impact of moderator variables on outcome is shown in the form of a diagram in Figure 6.1. Clearly, the greater the number of positive environmental moderators that can be set in place for a child by their parents and teachers, the better that child's outcome will be – so having their difficulties identified early on, receiving high-quality teaching and intervention, recognizing additional risks, having accommodations put in place for them at school, receiving lots of support at home, and being given encouragement and praise will provide the child with the best chance of doing well at school and in later life.

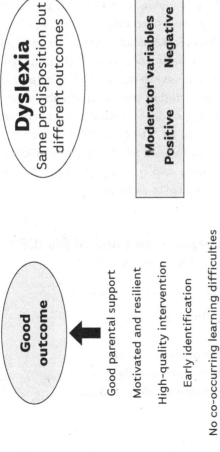

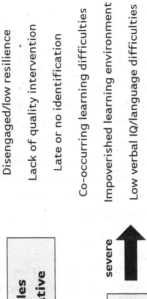

Poor outcome

Low parental support

Disengaged/low resilience

Lack of quality intervention

Late or no identification

Co-occurring learning difficulties

Impoverished learning environment

Low verbal IQ/language difficulties

Dyslexia

Same predisposition but different outcomes

Moderator variables

Positive   Negative

severe

Phonological deficit

mild

Genetic/neurodevelopmental predisposition

Good outcome

Good parental support

Motivated and resilient

High-quality intervention

Early identification

No co-occurring learning difficulties

Stimulating learning environment

High verbal IQ/good language

Figure 6.1: Dyslexia: Same predisposition but different outcomes

LET'S RECAP

- Following the assessment, teachers and parents should receive face-to-face feedback and of course a written report which provides a formulation (or diagnosis), together with detailed recommendations for how the child's difficulties should be remediated and managed.
- It is important in assessments to not just look at the child's difficulties but their strengths too, and to go beyond test scores to consider moderator variables (cognitive, personal and environmental) that influence progress and outcome.

What we'll do now is to use what we've discussed so far in this chapter to describe the assessments (and also one of the IEPs) of Alex, who was introduced in Chapter 4. Recall that he is a child who initially presented at age six with early speech and language delay and who then went on to develop severe dyslexia. Alex's (and our other cases') test scores are provided in the form of tables which you might expect to see in the Appendix of a report. Skim through or skip over the test scores if you find these a bit too technical. I wanted to include them to show you what they look like and to reassure you that the summary and formulation I produce are based on the evidence that these tests provide.

Alex's assessments, his reports and one of his IEPs

Box 6.3 describes Alex's test profile at age six.

Box 6.3: Alex's test results at age six

- WPPSI IV (an IQ test for three- to six-year-olds, with two cognitive scales):
  - Verbal Comprehension Index/Verbal IQ = 81

- - Visual Spatial Index/Non-verbal IQ = 114
- WIAT-III (an educational attainment test that includes some diagnostic measures):
  - Single Word Reading – standard score = 75
  - Pseudoword (non-word) Decoding – standard score = 60
  - Spelling – standard score = 70
  - Numeracy – standard score = 110
  - Maths Problem Solving – standard score = 90
  - Repeating Sentences – standard score = 80
- YARC (a passage reading test – the child reads a passage out loud and then orally answers questions on its content):
  - Reading Accuracy – standard score = 80
  - Reading Comprehension – standard score = 80
- CTOPP-2 (a diagnostic test for dyslexia and related language difficulties, with phonological awareness, naming speed and auditory working memory tests):
  - Blending Words – scaled score = 8
  - Elision (phoneme deletion) – scaled score = 6
  - Memory for Digits – scaled score = 6
  - Rapid Colour Naming – scaled score = 6
  - Non-word Repetition – scaled score = 7
- Visual Motor and Writing Skills:
  - Beery Test of Visuomotor Integration – standard score = 105
  - Handwriting – good letter formation, legible printing script.

NB: Standard scores have a mean (or average) of 100 while scaled scores have a mean of 10.

Alex's report summary and formulation at age six

Let's first **summarize** Alex's learning and educational profile. Alex is a six-year-old boy who has above average non-verbal ability. However, he scored at a significantly lower level on the verbal ability tests. This discrepancy is what we would expect to see in a child with a developmental language disorder. Alex obtained extremely low scores on the tests of reading and spelling, especially the non-word reading test. He also has poor reading comprehension. Alex is making better progress in maths. He did very well on a pencil-and-paper test assessing his basic arithmetic skills, though less well on a test which taps into maths concepts and the 'language of maths'. His handwriting and his visual motor skills are progressing nicely. Alex performed weakly on the dyslexia-sensitive tests of phonological awareness, phonological processing and auditory working memory. Finally, Alex struggled with the tests that are markers of oral language difficulties.

How would we **formulate** Alex's difficulties? I would describe (or diagnose) him as a little boy of above average ability who has a developmental language disorder, together with emerging dyslexia. Alex's poor oral language would be expected to have far-reaching effects on his ability to learn in the classroom as he struggles to follow what his teacher tells the class. It also explains his reading comprehension difficulties. Alex's slow progress in learning to read and spell, his weak decoding and his phonological difficulties all point to him also having dyslexia. These two disorders co-occur because they share the same causes (weaknesses in phonological processing and phonological/auditory working memory). Alex did not show any attention difficulties during the test session and his visual motor and handwriting skills are well developed; we can therefore exclude his having co-occurring ADHD or dyspraxia. Alex showed signs of lack of confidence and even slight anxiety, presumably because he knows he is behind in literacy and because he finds it hard to understand what is being said in the classroom. Alex struggles a little with the language of maths which is due to his speech and language problems, though his general arithmetic computation skills are sound. There is a family history of literacy difficulties suggesting that Alex's co-occurring language and literacy difficulties are inherited.

After this first assessment, Alex's teachers went on to prepare his first IEP for addressing his literacy difficulties (see Box 6.4); see chapters 8 and 9 for details of the literacy intervention programmes used.

Box 6.4: Alex's IEP

Chronological age: Six years

Start date: 6 January

Review date: 6 April

Input: Three 20-minute sessions one-to-one (1:1) per week with the school's learning support assistant (LSA) with pro-grammes prescribed and monitored by the SENCo plus two 30-minute small-group literacy lessons with the SENCo.

Targets	Support strategies	Outcome criteria	Date criteria met
To orally blend and segment single syllable words	1:1 phonological awareness training	Can blend four-phoneme words and identify/ segment beginning and end sounds	20 Jan – three phoneme blends 4 Feb – segment beginning sounds 3 March – four phoneme blends 2 April – segment end sounds
To decode two-, three- and four-letter words	Small group and 1:1 phonics lessons with real and non-words	Can decode five new or five non-words in a row correctly at each level	26 Jan – two-letter words 7 March – three-letter words 3 April – four-letter words
To learn ten common irregular words	Small-group lessons using SOS (say, cover, write, check)	Able to spell all ten words correctly to dictation	2 Feb – five words 28 March – ten words
To read four short books per week	1:1 listening to him read	Reading all four books accurately and fluently	15 Feb – two books 2 April – four books
To spell three- and four-letter words	Small group phonic approach to spelling and *Word shark*	Able to spell seven words of each length to dictation	4–15 March – all words learned

Other agencies involved: Speech and language therapist who visits the school twice per month to check on oral language progress and to advise parents, teachers and SENCo on how they can promote Alex's language skills.

Alex's second or follow-up assessment took place when he was 13. The test results are given in Box 6.5.

Box 6.5: Alex's test results at age 13

- WISC-V (an IQ test for 6- to 16-year-olds, with five cognitive scales):
  - Verbal Comprehension Index/Verbal IQ = 92
  - Visual Spatial Index/Non-verbal IQ = 114
  - Fluid Reasoning Index = 115
  - Auditory Working Memory Index = 84
  - Processing Speed Index = 100
- WIAT-III (an educational attainment test that includes some diagnostic measures):
  - Single Word Reading – standard score = 82
  - Pseudoword (non-word) Decoding – standard score = 70
  - Spelling – standard score = 72
  - Numeracy – standard score = 105
  - Maths Problem Solving – standard score = 90
  - Repeating Sentences – standard score = 84
- YARC (a passage reading test – child reads silently to themselves while being timed and then answers orally questions on the content):
  - Reading Speed – standard score = 75
  - Reading Comprehension – standard score = 90
- CTOPP-2 (a diagnostic test for dyslexia and associated language difficulties, with phonological awareness, naming speed and auditory working memory tests):

- Elision – scaled score = 9
- Rapid Letter Naming – scaled score = 5
- Non-word Repetition – scaled score = 6
- Detailed Assessment of Speed of Handwriting (DASH):
  - Free Writing Speed – standard score = 70; content poor, with grammatical errors evident and a limited range of vocabulary used.

Alex's report summary and formulation at age 13

Summarizing the results of this new assessment, we can see that Alex continues to present as a young man of above average non-verbal ability. Although his verbal abilities are still lower than his non-verbal abilities, he has nonetheless shown definite improvements in his oral language skills (his Verbal Comprehension Index score has risen from 81 when he was aged six to a current 92, which is within normal limits). However, reading, writing and spelling remain considerable challenges for Alex; he scored at a well below average level on measures of word reading, speed of reading, phonic decoding, spelling and speed of writing. His reading comprehension has developed quite well alongside his improvements in oral language. Alex's maths continues to be a relative strength, especially his computation skills, although some difficulties with the language of maths remain (he finds word problem solving hard). Alex's phonological awareness has improved a little through speech and language therapy and literacy intervention, although his phonological processing remains slow and inefficient. Alex still registers on the markers of DLD even though improvements in his oral language skills have taken place.

What is Alex's current **formulation**? Alex is an intelligent young man with a history of speech and language delay and a diagnosis of developmental language disorder. His oral language skills have improved in response to intensive speech and language therapy, and are now within normal limits for his age. Having said that, some mild residual language difficulties remain; his vocabulary knowledge, his reading comprehension, his written narrative and his understanding of the language of maths are relatively weak. Alex's primary difficulty is now his severe dyslexia, which is affecting all components of literacy skill, with his progress being noticeably slow. In spite of this, his teachers report that he is a motivated and cheerful young man who concentrates well and who works hard. He is said to be doing well in science, art and Computer Aided Design (CAD), as well as holding his own in maths.

KEY MESSAGES TO TAKE AWAY

✓ It is possible to identify children with literacy and related language difficulties by looking at their family history and developmental history (especially pre-school language) and through using observations and screening tests of oral language skill, spoken vocabulary, alphabet knowledge and phonological/phonic skill.

✓ Children who are making slow progress in literacy need to be monitored closely and provided with classroom support and targeted programmes aimed at improving their literacy skills.

✓ Children who fail to progress even with additional support may require a more comprehensive assessment of their learning difficulties and their profile of strength and weakness – so that more individually tailored interventions and management plans can be put in place for them.

Chapter 7

Identifying and Assessing Co-occurring Difficulties

In this chapter I describe how:

→ class teachers can look out for signs that indicate that their pupil might have not just dyslexia but also a co-occurring difficulty in arithmetic, attention or handwriting

→ difficulties of maths, attention and handwriting need also to be assessed, alongside those of literacy – the assessment of co-occurring difficulties usually takes the form of testing but also observations and rating scales can be used, especially when a child has attention and/or behaviour problems

→ assessments of co-occurring difficulties are carried out and the findings added to the diagnostic formulation of a child with literacy difficulties – illustrating this with the case studies introduced in Chapter 5

→ we assess a second language learner who is making slow progress in developing spoken and written English.

In the previous chapter, we looked at identifying and assessing the child with dyslexia who also has an accompanying language difficulty. In this chapter, I concentrate on identifying and assessing the child who has dyslexia co-occurring with a **simultaneous** learning difficulty: specific arithmetic disorder/dyscalculia, attention problems/ADHD or visual motor/handwriting difficulties. This is illustrated by revisiting the children introduced in Chapter 5 and describing how their difficulties were assessed. I also talk a little more about assessing the child who is a second language learner.

A case study of Susanna illustrates how we assess a bilingual child who is struggling to learn to read in English.

Could my pupil have a co-occurring learning difficulty and what do I do about it?

★ Checklist (downloadable from www.jkp.com/catalogue/book/9781839977046)

Could my pupil have dyscalculia/specific arithmetic disorder, as well as literacy difficulties? Five key questions to ask (tick YES or NO as appropriate):

	YES	NO
In the first three years at school:		
1. Does the child have trouble learning new concepts in maths?	☐	☐
2. Do they get confused while counting numbers?	☐	☐
3. Do they count on their fingers, even when working with very small numbers?	☐	☐
4. Are they finding it hard to learn the basic number bonds to 10 without resorting to their fingers every time (e.g. '2 + 2 = 4', '3 + 4 = 7')?	☐	☐
5. Do they struggle to compare number size (e.g. 'Which is the bigger number, 2 or 5 ?')?	☐	☐
By Years 3–6 (and even on into the secondary school years):		
1. Does the child have trouble learning new concepts in maths?	☐	☐
2. Are they still struggling with the basic number bonds and still counting on their fingers a lot?	☐	☐

	YES	NO
3. Do they struggle to remember how to do the basic number operations, especially addition with 'carry-over' and subtraction with 'payback'?	☐	☐
4. Do they 'lose their place' while they're working through a sum?	☐	☐
5. Are they anxious about maths, feel they're 'rubbish' at it and often rush through their maths exercises 'to get them out the way'?	☐	☐

If you've answered yes to at least three of the questions in either section your pupil could have a specific arithmetic difficulty or dyscalculia.

Could my pupil have ADHD, as well as literacy difficulties?

	YES	NO
1. Does the child have a very short concentration span?	☐	☐
2. Are they easily distracted?	☐	☐
3. Are they very 'daydreamy' and 'switched off'?	☐	☐
4. Are they very active, impulsive and 'all over the place'?	☐	☐
5. Do they fidget a lot and find it hard to sit still?	☐	☐
6. Do they find it hard to settle down to start tasks – and to finish them without walking away?	☐	☐

If you've answered yes to at least three of these questions, your pupil could have ADHD. However, do bear in mind that many children in their early primary years are still settling into school life and routines. We sometimes see children who are poor at concentrating, fidgety and distractible during the first two or three years at school, but settle thereafter. It is important therefore to see how the fidgety and distractible four- to seven-year-old gets on as they move into Year 3 – without becoming too alarmed. But if they are still not improving in their concentration by age eight, it is definitely worth taking matters further.

Could my pupil have developmental coordination disorder (DCD)/dyspraxia, as well as literacy difficulties? Five key questions to ask (some of these will need to draw on information from parents):

	YES	NO
In the first two to three years at school:		
1. Was the child late to walk?	☐	☐
2. Did they struggle to learn how to use a spoon, knife and fork?	☐	☐
3. Do they find drawing shapes and people figures difficult?	☐	☐
4. Do they struggle with forming letters when handwriting?	☐	☐
5. Are they clumsy and do they find ball games difficult?	☐	☐
By Years 3–6 (and even on into the secondary school years):		
1. Is the child still struggling to form letters when handwriting?	☐	☐
2. Have they found it hard to move from printing to cursive (joined-up) writing?	☐	☐
3. Is their handwriting messy and untidy?	☐	☐

4. Do they have trouble drawing diagrams, graphs and charts? ☐ ☐

5. Are they slow to complete writing activities? ☐ ☐

If you've answered yes to at least three of the questions in either section, your pupil could have DCD/dyspraxia.

What you should do about it

Essentially you need to follow the steps recommended in the previous chapter:

- Approach the child's parent/carer and discuss your concerns with them.
- Work together on a plan of action.
- Involve the school's SENCo.
- See if a more detailed assessment of their learning and their literacy difficulties is required.

Assessing the child with a literacy and co-occurring difficulty

The principles of assessment laid out in Chapter 6 apply just as much here. The assessment for literacy and co-occurring difficulties will still include cognitive (IQ) measures, tests of educational attainment and diagnostic tests of dyslexia. But some additional tests will be needed to see if your pupil has co-occurring dyscalculia, ADHD or DCD/dyspraxia.

Tests of co-occurring specific learning difficulties

Dyscalculia-sensitive tests, on which children with arithmetic difficulties tend to do badly, measure:

- numerosity (number sense)
- short-term auditory/verbal working memory
- visual spatial ability (sometimes)
- speed of carrying out simple arithmetic items.

135

Tests that are **ADHD sensitive** are rather less useful because this is a complex difficulty which is perhaps best understood through:

- gathering information from interviews, standardized questionnaires and rating scales completed by parents and teachers; these typically ask parents and teachers to answer questions or to rate where the child stands in relation to behaviours such as:
  - inattention
  - hyperactivity/impulsivity
  - ability to inhibit (or hold back)
  - ability to self-monitor (or keep track of their performance or the effect of their own behaviour)
  - initiating (starting) activities
  - ability to shift attention when required
- structured observation of the child's concentration and behaviour within the classroom.

Having said that, there are some specific standardized tests that assess children's ability to **sustain** and to **switch** attention. It is also useful to look at the child's processing speed because as we saw earlier children with ADHD are frequently slow and inefficient information processors.

Dyspraxia-sensitive tests, on which children with visual motor problems do badly, measure:

- non-verbal ability
- visual perception, fine motor and visual motor integration skills
- motor organization
- timed pencil-and-paper copying and visual scanning skills.

LET'S RECAP

- As a class teacher, you can identify whether a pupil might have a co-occurring learning difficulty by asking questions about their classroom performance

136

and behaviour which would suggest that they have arithmetic, attention or motor problems.
- Diagnostic measures for co-occurring learning difficulties include tests of numerosity and visual spatial skill (arithmetic disorders/dyscalculia), attention rating scales and questionnaires (ADHD) and tests of visual motor integration and organization (dyspraxia).

Let's now look at what an assessment and its accompanying report looks like for each of the children introduced in Chapter 5 – Jyoti, who has dyslexia and co-occurring arithmetic disorder/dyscalculia; Billy, who has dyslexia and co-occurring attention disorder; and Freddie, who has dyslexia and co-occurring visual motor disorder/ DCD (dyspraxia).

Co-occurring arithmetic disorder/dyscalculia – Jyoti's assessment and formulation

Recall from Chapter 5 that Jyoti is a nine-year-old girl referred because of concerns about her spelling and written output skills, her slow processing and her weak maths. Jyoti's test scores are given in Box 7.1.

Remember that index and standard scores have a mean (or average) of 100, while scaled scores have a mean of 10.

Box 7.1: Jyoti's test results

- WISC-V (an IQ test for 6- to 16-year-olds, with five cognitive scales):
  - Verbal Comprehension Index/Verbal IQ = 111
  - Visual Spatial Index = 86
  - Fluid Reasoning Index = 88
  - Auditory Working Memory Index = 85
  - Processing Speed Index = 106

- WIAT-III (an educational attainment test that includes some diagnostic measures):
  - Single Word Reading – standard score = 103
  - Pseudoword (non-word) Decoding – standard score = 105
  - Spelling – standard score = 88
  - Numeracy – standard score = 90
  - Maths Problem Solving – standard score = 80
- YARC (a passage reading test – child reads a passage out loud while being timed and then orally answers questions on the content):
  - Reading Accuracy – standard score = 104
  - Reading Speed – standard score = 105
  - Reading Comprehension – standard score = 116
- CTOPP-2 (a diagnostic test for dyslexia, with phonological awareness, naming speed and auditory working memory tests):
  - Elision – scaled score = 5
  - Rapid Letter Naming – scaled score = 6
- Detailed Assessment of Speed of Handwriting (DASH):
  - Free Writing Speed – standard score = 100; fair expression of ideas, sentence constructions and vocabulary usage
- Test of Basic Arithmetic and Numeracy Skills (TOBANS) (contains tests that assess numerosity):
  - Dot Comparison – standard score = 79
  - Count the Dots – standard score = 89
  - Digit Comparison – standard score = 90

Jyoti's report summary and formulation

Jyoti is a little girl of slightly above average verbal intelligence who does therefore have the language skills to support good educational development. In fact, literacy testing indicates that she is doing well in reading. She achieved average to above average scores on tests of single-word reading, passage reading accuracy, reading comprehension, reading speed and phonic decoding. She is, however, a rather weak speller. Her mathematical skills are below the level to be expected for a girl of her age who is also verbally able. Her handwriting is a nicely formed mix of printing and cursive scripts and she writes at an average speed for her age. Her written expression skills are developing well.

Jyoti is a verbally able girl who has a specific learning difficulty that is made up of two disorders: dyslexia and dyscalculia (specific arithmetic disorder). Typical of children with dyslexia, Jyoti displays underlying phonological awareness and processing difficulties, and also a weak phonological/auditory working memory. However, her phonic decoding is better than we would expect, given her weak phonological skills. This suggests that she has responded well to the targeted phonic decoding programmes that have been delivered both in and out of school. Jyoti's improved decoding has fuelled her recent good progress in reading, although spelling difficulties remain. Jyoti's dyscalculia is associated with poor visual perceptual and spatial skills and weak numerosity. Another difficulty that is causing Jyoti's struggle with maths is her weak short-term auditory working memory, which impairs her mental maths and her ability to retain number facts like multiplication tables.

Dyslexia and dyscalculia are two specific learning difficulties that commonly co-occur because they share a common 'risk' or cause: a short-term auditory working memory weakness. Also, recall that Jyoti was rather delayed in her early language development, a feature often found in children with co-occurring literacy and arithmetic difficulties. It is important to note that Jyoti has definite strengths in respect of her now good verbal abilities, her advanced reading skills and her high levels of motivation.

We will revisit Jyoti's case for the final time when we look at her intervention plan in Chapter 10.

Co-occurring ADHD – Billy's assessment and formulation

In Chapter 5, I introduced Billy, a seven-year-old boy who is competent in reading and maths but making slow progress in spelling and written work. His parents and teachers also expressed concern about his lack of concentration and his restless and distracted behaviour. Billy's test scores are given in Box 7.2.

Box 7.2: Billy's test results

- WISC-V (an IQ test for 6- to 16-year-olds, with five cognitive scales):
  - Verbal Comprehension Index/Verbal IQ = 127
  - Visual Spatial Index/Non-verbal IQ = 135
  - Fluid Reasoning Index = 134
  - Auditory Working Memory Index = 91
  - Processing Speed Index = 89
- WIAT-III (an educational attainment test that includes some diagnostic measures):
  - Single Word Reading – standard score = 100
  - Pseudoword Decoding – standard score = 90
  - Spelling – standard score = 95
  - Numeracy – standard score = 110
  - Maths Problem Solving – standard score = 115
  - Written Expression – able to write simple sentences of his own.
- YARC (a passage reading test – child reads a passage out loud while being timed and then orally answers questions on the content):
  - Reading Accuracy – standard score = 111
  - Reading Speed – standard score = 108
  - Reading Comprehension – standard score = 123
- CTOPP-2 (a diagnostic test for dyslexia, with phonological awareness, naming speed and auditory working memory tests):
  - Elision – scaled score = 11
  - Rapid Letter Naming – scaled score = 7
- Test of Everyday Attention for Children (TEA-Ch2) (a computerized test of sustained attention and switching attention):

- Sustained Attention – scaled score = 6
- Switching Attention – scaled score = 7

Billy's report summary and formulation

Billy is a very intelligent and articulate young man and we would expect him to perform educationally at a high level. In fact, his test scores reveal that he is a competent mathematician. Although his single-word reading vocabulary is average for his age, it is unexpectedly weak for so able a child. He does, however, read well in prose context. His speed of reading is fair, and he has good reading comprehension. There are, however, insecurities in his phonic decoding ability. His spelling is within the normal range for his age but definitely below ability expectation. In handwriting, he shows good letter formation and he is beginning to develop simple written expression skills. Because of concerns about Billy's concentration, his parents and teachers were asked to complete an attention rating scale, the Conners Attention Questionnaire. Of the six subscales of the Conners, Billy scored within the 'clinical concern' range on three of these, specifically on hyperactivity/impulsivity, inattention and executive function.

Billy is a very bright and articulate boy who has a lot of academic potential which he fulfils across a wide range of classroom subjects – oral classwork, reading comprehension, maths and handwriting. However, he does show signs of mild dyslexia; there are gaps in his single-word reading, his phonic decoding skills are insecure, his spelling is relatively weak, his auditory working memory is below ability expectation and his phonological processing is poor. He is developing compensatory strategies – note that his passage reading accuracy is stronger than his single-word reading and he has very good reading comprehension, indicating that he is making good use of context and is also taking advantage of his excellent oral vocabulary. Billy's dyslexia is fortunately mild, given that he 'gets by' in reading and his spelling difficulties are relatively minor. Co-occurring alongside the dyslexia are attention problems. His scores on the TEA-Ch 2 were low, and during the test session he found it hard to focus and he was also rather restless, fidgety and distractible. Additionally, he scored within the 'clinical concern' range on three out of six subscales of the Conners Questionnaire. As is often the case for children with attention problems, Billy is a slow processor. Billy shows definite strengths in his verbal and non-verbal abilities, his reading comprehension and his maths. These function as **protective** factors which will help improve his educational outcome.

We will revisit Billy in Chapter 10 when we look at his intervention plan.

Co-occurring DCD/dyspraxia – Freddie's assessment and formulation

In Chapter 5, I introduced Freddie, a 12-year-old boy with a long-standing history of literacy difficulties who has shown recent improvements in his reading but who has a lot of difficulty in expressing himself on paper. His handwriting is often illegible, he is slow to complete writing tasks and his written work is viewed by his teachers as untidy and often inaccurate and incoherent. Freddie's parents are becoming concerned about his moodiness and occasional angry outbursts. His teachers view him as lacking in motivation. Freddie's test scores are summarized in Box 7.3.

Box 7.3: Freddie's test results

- WISC-V (an IQ test for 6- to 16-year-olds, with five cognitive scales):
  - Verbal Comprehension Index/Verbal IQ = 111
  - Visual Spatial Index/Nonverbal IQ = 86
  - Fluid Reasoning Index = 109
  - Auditory Working Memory Index = 88
  - Processing Speed Index = 83
- WIAT-III (an educational attainment test that includes some diagnostic measures):
  - Single Word Reading – standard score = 90
  - Oral Reading Speed – standard score = 85
  - Spelling – standard score = 79

- Numeracy – standard score = 105
- Maths Problem Solving – standard score = 110
- YARC Secondary (a passage reading test – child reads a passage silently while being timed and then answers questions on the content):
  - Reading Speed – standard score = 95
  - Reading Comprehension – standard score = 112
- CTOPP2 (a diagnostic test for dyslexia, with phonological awareness, naming speed and auditory working memory tests):
  - Elision – scaled score = 9
  - Rapid Letter Naming – scaled score = 3
- Test of Word Reading Efficiency (TOWRE-2) (lists of 'real' sight words and non-words scored for both accuracy and speed):
  - Sight Word Efficiency – standard score = 71
  - Phonemic Decoding Efficiency – standard score = 73
- Detailed Assessment of Speed of Handwriting (DASH):
  - Free Writing Standard score = 100; fair expression of ideas, sentence constructions and vocabulary usage
- Beery Test of Visuomotor Integration and Rey Complex Figure Copy Test (copy drawing tests of visual motor integration and motor organization skill) – standard scores of 80 and 75 respectively

Freddie's report summary and formulation

Freddie is a young man of above average verbal intelligence and we would expect him to be doing well in classroom learning. Freddie is indeed a competent mathematician. He is, however, struggling with some aspects of reading. There are gaps in his word vocabulary, he is a slow reader and his phonic decoding is weak. His reading comprehension is good. Freddie is a poor speller. His handwriting shows uneven letter formation and can at times be difficult to read. He holds the pen incorrectly and he also writes very slowly. His written sentence constructions and vocabulary were noted to be immature for a verbally able student. Freddie appeared at times rather disengaged during the assessment; this showed as being 'off hand' in his manner, looking bored and giving up all too readily when he found an activity challenging. Freddie's parents and teachers were asked to complete a behaviour questionnaire, the Strengths and Difficulties Questionnaire. His scores on this scale were within the 'clinical concern' range on the Emotional Symptoms and Conduct Problem Scales.

Freddie is an able young man whose profile is indicative of his having dyslexia. He struggles with word-level reading, phonic decoding and spelling – all clear signs of dyslexia. He also displays the phonological/auditory working memory and phonological processing weaknesses that are seen in students with this disorder. Freddie's reading has improved of late in response to the intervention he has had, and he may well have developed some compensatory strategies (through his good language skills). Certainly, his **functional** reading skills (his reading comprehension and his speed of reading silently to himself) are within the normal range. But he reads out loud slowly and he is a poor speller. Co-occurring alongside the dyslexia are visual spatial, motor organization and visual processing difficulties that are consistent with his having DCD/dyspraxia. His DCD accounts for his struggles with handwriting speed and quality and also his generally poor written presentation and organization. Freddie's long-term educational struggles have caused him increasing frustration over the years, which is now resulting in moodiness and angry outbursts at home and disengagement in lessons at school.

We will meet up with Freddie again in Chapter 10 when we look at his intervention plan.

Assessing literacy and language difficulties in second language learners

In the last chapter, I raised (albeit briefly) the challenges of assessing a child who is struggling to read but for whom English is not their mother tongue. This is an educational reality for increasing numbers of children, whether due to greater global mobility, immigration or multiculturalism. Revisit Box 6.2 to remind your-self about features of second language learners. Let's now look at Susanna, who is originally French speaking and whose parents have moved to the UK where she is now learning English and being educated in a local primary school.

SUSANNA: AN INTRODUCTION

Susanna is a nine-year-old girl who was referred for assessment by her parents and her teachers because of concerns about her slow academic progress. She was born in France and both parents are French speaking. She attended local French schools up until the age of seven years when her family relocated to the UK because of her father's job. Susanna found the transition to a country with a different language, culture and educational system very challenging. She started in Year 2 at her local state primary school and has had EAL (English as an Additional Language) instruction for the last two years.

Her progress in developing spoken English has not been as rapid as expected and she struggles to express herself in grammatically complete sentences, although her comprehension of English seems to be more secure. French continues to be the primary language spoken at home and Susanna attends French lessons on Saturday mornings. Her teachers in her French school have commented on her lack of vocabulary breadth in her mother tongue and her difficulty in learning to read and write in French. At her English school, Susanna is observed to concentrate well and she is a hard worker. She appears quite confident in maths (apart from some difficulty in under-standing word problems), and her handwriting is neat. She is, however, struggling to learn to read and spell in English, so, now in Year 4, she has recently commenced targeted literacy intervention, which includes phonics instruction.

Susanna's parents recall that her speech and language was slow to develop during her pre-school years; she was assessed at age three by a speech and language therapist who acknowledged her delay but did not think that therapy was indicated. Susanna is a healthy girl. There is a family history on her father's side of poor spelling.

Susanna's test results are shown in Box 7.4.

Box 7.4: Susanna's test results

- WISC-V (an IQ test for 6- to 16-year-olds, with five cognitive scales):
  - Verbal Comprehension Index/Verbal IQ = 86
  - Visual Spatial Index/Non-verbal IQ = 119
  - Fluid Reasoning Index = 118
  - Auditory Working Memory Index = 84
  - Processing Speed Index = 111
- WIAT-III (an educational attainment test that includes some diagnostic measures):
  - Single Word Reading – standard score = 85
  - Pseudoword Decoding – standard score = 75
  - Spelling – standard score = 72
  - Numeracy – standard score = 110
  - Maths Problem Solving – standard score = 90
  - Repeating Sentences – standard score = 84
- YARC (a passage reading test – the child reads a passage out loud while being timed and then orally answers questions on the content):
  - Reading Accuracy – standard score = 90
  - Reading Speed – standard score = 75
  - Reading Comprehension – standard score = 85
- CTOPP-2 (a diagnostic test for dyslexia, with phonological awareness, naming speed and auditory working memory tests):
  - Elision – scaled score = 7
  - Rapid Letter Naming – scaled score = 8
  - Non-word Repetition – scaled score = 7
- Detailed Assessment of Speed of Handwriting (DASH):
  - Free Writing Speed Standard score = 80; content

---

poor, with grammatical errors evident and
limited range of vocabulary used

Susanna's report summary and formulation

Susanna is a little girl of above average intelligence when assessed non-verbally. Her lower scores on the WISC-V Verbal Comprehension Scale subtests reflect her relative weakness in oral language, with her vocabulary knowledge being especially poor. Susanna is making good progress in her numeracy development; her slightly lower score on Maths Problem Solving is likely to be due to her weak word problem solving (reflecting struggles with the language of maths). Susanna is making slow progress in developing word-level reading and spelling skills and she reads and writes slowly. Her reading comprehension is especially poor.

Susanna is an able little girl whose test profile is consistent with her having a developmental language disorder (DLD), together with co-occurring dyslexia. Susanna struggled to acquire her mother tongue of French as a pre-schooler and even now shows some difficulties in expressing herself in this language. She has made slower than expected progress in acquiring English as a second language in spite of receiving EAL for two years. Susanna recorded low-average to below average scores on tests known to be 'markers' for language impairment (Nonword Repetition and Repeating Sentences). Co-occurring alongside the language disorder is developmental dyslexia. In contrast to most bilingual children, Susanna has made slow progress in acquiring word-level reading and spelling skills (and also phonological awareness). Indeed, she exhibits phonological processing, auditory working memory and decoding problems that are characteristic of a child with dyslexia. There is a positive family history of literacy problems. Susanna's reading comprehension difficulties are most likely due to her poor oral language skills, in particular her limited vocabulary knowledge. Language disorders and dyslexia commonly co-occur and of course in Susanna's case the educational expression of her learning difficulty is likely to be made worse (though not caused) by her French-English bilingualism.

We will meet Susanna again when we look at her intervention plan in the next chapter.

KEY MESSAGES TO TAKE AWAY

✓ When a child is referred with literacy difficulties, it is important to also consider whether they might have a simultaneous co-occurring difficulty such as a maths, attention or visual motor/handwriting problem; the assessment of these sorts of difficulties should still start with cognitive, educational and dyslexia-sensitive tests, but additional tests (and observations too) will be needed to see if they have a co-occurring learning difficulty that is important not to miss.

✓ To assess if a child has a specific arithmetic difficulty (or dyscalculia), tests of numerosity (number sense), auditory/verbal working memory and visual spatial abilities can be given.

✓ Assessing if a child has ADHD usually involves drawing on parent and teacher observations and concerns, but rating scales and even specific tests of aspects of attention (like ability to sustain concentration) can also be given; processing speed tests may be useful too, given that most children with ADHD are slow and inefficient processors.

✓ Measures of visual spatial, visual motor and motor organization abilities can help to decide whether a child's struggles with handwriting speed and written presentation are because of co-occurring DCD/dyspraxia.

✓ The assessment of second language learners who are slow to acquire oral and written English language skills should not be delayed; many of these children have underlying learning difficulties, most usually developmental language disorder and/or dyslexia.

Chapter 8

How We Teach Children with Literacy Difficulties

In this chapter I describe how:

→ children with dyslexia need a systematic intervention programme that teaches them phonological awareness and letter knowledge and how to build up words through phonics

→ reading rapidly and fluently is a challenge for most dyslexic children, who require lots of reading practice over long periods of time

→ older dyslexic children can improve their spelling by moving beyond spelling phonically to learning about larger word units (like special word endings) that are more reliably and consistently spelled

→ children with reading comprehension and associated language difficulties need teaching that enables them to improve their vocabulary, their comprehension and their ability to express themselves at both the oral language and text-based levels

→ biological therapies (like tinted lenses and motor exercises) that are sometimes recommended to treat reading problems do not have a strong scientific basis – and studies have shown that they rarely lead to sustained improvements in literacy skill.

By this stage of the book, you as a class teacher have learned a lot about what literacy difficulties are, what causes them and how they are expressed in the individual child. Chapter 6 looked at screening and assessing for literacy difficulties. So you have now reached the point where you know your pupil has a literacy difficulty; you have observed them and asked yourself questions about how they are performing in literacy, you have talked to their parents and the school's SENCo and some assessments have taken place that have confirmed your suspicions. So now we come to what happens next. How should this child be taught at school?

In this chapter, I describe teaching techniques that we know work best for children with literacy difficulties. Of course, teaching a child who has dyslexia (word-level reading difficulties) will be very different from teaching a child who has reading comprehension problems – so we look at these separately. I conclude this chapter by describing the personalized intervention plan of Alex, who has dyslexia occurring in the context of early speech and language delay, and of Susanna, a second language learner, who has both oral and written language difficulties. In the next chapter, I concentrate more specifically on what you can do as a class teacher to support your pupil within the classroom context.

How we teach children with dyslexia

In Part 1 of this book, I argued the case for dyslexia being caused by the child having underlying phonological processing difficulties that in turn make it hard for them to develop the phonic decoding strategies that are needed for learning to read. That being the case, it seems obvious that the teaching of dyslexic children needs to focus on helping them to become better phonological processors and phonic decoders – and that is exactly what dyslexic teaching programmes aim to do.

Training phonological skills

Phonological skills emerge naturally in typically developing children during the process of learning to talk as a pre-schooler, and become more refined and developed after they learn the alphabet during their first year of school. But this isn't the case for dyslexic children. They cannot easily acquire phonological awareness and phonological processing skills because they do not have the 'biological hardware' to do this (refresh your memory about the biological basis of dyslexia and the artificial intelligence/connectionist model talked about in Chapter 3). But there is good evidence to show that dyslexic children can be taught how to become phonologically aware and to process speech sounds in words – and this phonological teaching translates into improved reading skill.

What should be taught in a phonological training programme? Essentially, delivering such a programme involves carrying out auditory-based exercises that train children to blend, identify, segment and manipulate sounds in spoken words. For example, they might be asked to do the following:

- **Join sounds together to make a word** – for example, the teacher says the sounds 't', 'r', 'a', 'p' (spoken one second apart), 'What word do they make?' The child should respond 'trap.' The teacher starts with short and simple two-letter words and then moves to longer words.
- **Identify sounds in words** – for example, asking the child to tell them what is the first sound in a word, what is the end sound and what is the middle sound; for example, the first sound in the word 'cat' is 'c', the end sound is 't' and the middle sound is 'a'.
- **Segment sounds in words** – for example, the teacher says the first part of a word and then asks the child to 'finish it off'. 'Here is a picture of a cat. I'll say the beginning of the word, you finish it off' – the teacher says 'c' and the child responds 'at'.
- **Delete sounds in words** – the teacher asks the child to 'take away' the beginning or end sound of a word; for example, 'cat' without the 'c' says 'at', 'meet' without the 't' says 'mee'. Taking away middle sounds in words, like 'stick' without the 't' (says 'sick'), is much harder and needs to be worked on after the child has got to grips with deleting beginning and end sounds.

For all the activities above, teacher demonstration and regular practice with lots of different sounds and words are needed before the child is able to confidently process and analyse sounds in spoken words. Having said that, there is good evidence that phonological awareness training on its own is not sufficient to help children develop the skills needed to 'crack' the alphabetic code (see Chapters 1 and 3). Recall that I said earlier that for children to crack this code and to make the breakthrough to independent reading, three conditions need to be met:

1. The child needs to have a level of phonological skill that enables them to split spoken words into their constituent sounds (which is what the above phonological exercises aim to do).
2. They need to know the letters of the alphabet and their corresponding sounds.
3. They need to link these two skills together (phonological linkage).

So, alongside phonological training, the child needs to learn all 26 letters of the alphabet, how they are written and which sound corresponds with each letter. It is usual to teach the sounds of the letters first and then later on their names.

And then we come to phonological linkage – which is about teaching the child to link sounds to letters within the words they are learning to read. Exercises to help develop phonological linkage could involve the child doing the phonological activities described above while at the same time working with the letters that represent them. To do this, the child needs a set of alphabet letters (on flashcards or perhaps made of felt). So, for instance, in the case of the blending activity, the teacher says each sound slowly ('c-a-t') and asks the child to point to the relevant alphabet letters while also saying its corresponding sound – and then eventually blending the sounds to make the word 'cat'.

An example of a phonological training programme that is widely used and has been validated in research studies is Sound Linkage by Peter Hatcher, Fiona Duff and Charles Hulme (2014).

Teaching phonic decoding skills

Once the child is more phonologically aware and is able to reliably link letters and sounds, it is time to move on to a phonic-based teaching programme. You may recall that in Chapter 1 I mentioned a **synthetic phonics programme**, which, when applied systematically, works well for dyslexic children who have already established the basic phonological skills just described. Let's just recap on the description of synthetic phonics in Chapter 1:

> The 26 letter sounds are taught very quickly, six every eight days or so, using the whiteboard to show the printed letter, with the teacher demonstrating how to say the sound, while the children repeat what she says. The teacher shows how the sound is used in different words. There is lots of opportunity for practice and reviewing the sounds the children have learned at earlier lessons. The children then learn how to put the letter sounds together (i.e. they blend the sounds to make a word). So, after the children have been taught the letter sounds, the teacher shows them how to sound them out and blend them to make words – the early stage of phonic decoding. The children then write the letters they have learned and the word they have blended, ('c', 'a', 't' says 'cat'– perhaps accompanied by the child drawing a cat). Common exception words like 'he', 'the', 'was' are introduced at this stage, teaching them mainly as whole words as they are difficult to sound out and blend.
>
> Once the children have learned all the alphabet letter sounds and know how to blend them to make words and write simple two- and three-letter words, they are ready to learn about more complex sounds made up of two letters – 'ay', 'ou', 'ch', 'er' and so on. These are taught in the same way as the single letters, with lots of practice in saying the new sound, hearing it in whole words, blending sounds together to make words, learning how to write the letters that make up the sound and then writing them within whole words. The teacher asks the children to spell the new sound, sometimes out loud (orally) and then write the spelling as an activity at their desks. More complicated exception words like 'people' and 'because' are taught separately.

There is good evidence that synthetic phonics programmes work well for dyslexic children – but with three 'add-ons'.

- First, a synthetic phonics programme should be delivered

within a **multisensory teaching framework** that encourages the child to take advantage of all the sensory input routes to learning – that is, the auditory route through hearing and saying the sounds and words, the visual route through looking at written words and letter patterns, and the kinaesthetic route through writing letters and words.

- Second, phonics should not be 'skill and drill' – that is, not just doing the exercises described above; phonics needs to be taught alongside **whole-book reading**. So, as well as being taught phonics, children should be reading stories so that they come to appreciate that reading is not just about 'sounding out' printed words, but is also about understanding what they read, learning new things and enjoying stories.

- Finally, dyslexic children need lots of practice and reinforcement of sounds, letters, phonic sounding out and so on – more so than typically developing children. This is because it takes them longer to build up and consolidate the sound–letter connections (mappings) that come easily to the non-dyslexic child. And this is where parents and teaching assistants have a particularly important part to play because they are in a strong position to provide the necessary repetition and practice that the child needs to become a good reader.

Many dyslexic children who receive phonological training and systematic phonics and have lots of reading practice eventually come to read adequately. However, there are two aspects of literacy which provide a particular challenge for dyslexic children – reading rapidly and spelling. These are often long-term issues which can follow them well into their adolescence and even their adult life. So how do we address these?

The thorny problem of reading fast enough

Even when children with dyslexia come to read accurately, their speed and fluency usually lag behind. Being a slow and effortful reader disadvantages children in a number of ways. First, it means that they struggle in timed situations such as written exams; they can't read fast enough so they don't finish the exam paper. Second, it may adversely affect their reading comprehension because they 'lose track and fail to memorize' what they are reading. And finally, it can be sufficiently discouraging to result in them actively avoiding reading activities. Teaching strategies that are designed to specifically target reading speed and fluency usually involve some form of guided repeated oral reading, an example of which is **repeated reading intervention.** Typically, the child reads the same segment of text out loud over and over again until they reach an acceptable level of fluency (after which they move on to a different text). Research studies have shown that this training results in quite large improvements in reading speed (and also to some extent reading comprehension). Repeated reading intervention is probably most realistically carried out either by teaching assistants, classroom volunteers or by parents at home, as class teachers and SENCos rarely have the time to devote to near-daily listening to children read. I describe this approach in more detail in the next chapter when I talk about what you as a classroom teacher can do to advise and support teaching assistants, classroom volunteers and parents on how to deliver a reading speed/ fluency programme.

And spelling is even more of a problem!

Most dyslexic children are at risk of having persisting spelling difficulties, even though they may have responded well to a systematic phonological/phonic teaching programme and achieved a reasonable level of reading accuracy. Spelling in English provides an especial challenge because it is complex and is based on units that go beyond simple sound-to-letter mappings.

Because spelling, like reading, is phonic-based, a spelling programme needs to begin with phonological awareness training and the learning of letter names and sounds. **Graphemes** are how we represent phonemes as written letters. We start with simple graphemes that are just single letters and then we move on to more complex graphemes that are letter combinations – such as consonant clusters (e.g. bl, st, fr), digraphs (e.g. sh, th, ch) and diphthongs (e.g. oo, ea, ou, oi). Spelling patterns like these need to be presented in a systematic order, only one pattern should be

155

introduced at a time, and patterns previously taught should be regularly revised.

Dyslexic children need to spend a lot of time learning **key words**. These are high-frequency words such as **was**, **in**, **of**, **me**, **because**. It has been estimated that just 12 words make up 25 per cent of everything we read and write: a, and, he, it, of, that, I, in, is, the, to, was. And there are a further 88 words that make up half of the total words we write — words like but, because, on, down. Unfortunately, many key words are irregularly spelled (e.g. could, when, some, said) but, because of their importance, they need to be taught early. A fuller list of key word spellings is provided in the next chapter. A commonly used approach to teaching key words is **Simultaneous Oral Spelling (SOS)**. Put simply, the child looks at the printed word, hears and speaks it as a whole word, names the individual letters out loud and then writes the word. The word is covered and written again from memory, with the process repeated several times.

Many spelling programmes emphasize teaching at the smallest unit level, i.e. the grapheme. However, we have seen that many dyslexic children have great difficulty in learning and remembering grapheme–phoneme connections. A particular problem is that the spelling of graphemes at this small unit level is often highly inconsistent and irregular. It is suggested, therefore, that we need to supplement phonic spelling programmes with teaching strategies that encourage the child to focus on larger units in words. One of the advantages of this approach for dyslexic children is that it reduces the load on the processing and memorizing of lengthy phoneme sequences (which they find difficult because of their auditory working memory weakness). Additionally, there is good evidence that larger units in words (like morphemes, which are described shortly) show greater spelling consistency and regularity than do smaller unit graphemes. It follows, therefore, that it should be easier for the dyslexic child to learn and to use these larger letter units without being confused by the many exceptions that are seen at the smaller unit level.

An example of a large unit teaching approach in spelling is that of **analogy** (teachers and parents may be more familiar with the term 'word families'). An analogy involves using the spelling-sound pattern of a known word, for instance 'beak' to spell an unknown word which shares the same spelling pattern, such as 'peak'. In this example, the initial letter is called the onset ('b' or 'p') and the following letters the rime ('eak'). Examples of rimes which have many onsets and which enable children to predict the spelling of a large number of words include: **ang** (as in fang, bang, sang), **end** (as in bend, send, mend), **ight** (as in fight, sight, slight, might), and **ay** (as in may, stay, lay).

There is also evidence to suggest that teaching children about morphemes (units of meaning) can improve their spelling (Nunes and Bryant, 2009). The most common morphemes that are taught to help children spell are prefixes at the beginning of words and suffixes at the end of words. Examples of prefixes are beginning morphemes that make negatives (e.g. **un-**, **dis-**, as in '**un**interest-ing', '**dis**abled') and the prefix **re** as in '**re**apply', '**re**sume'. Examples of suffixes are **-y** endings that can form adjectives (as in 'thirst**y**', 'funn**y**') or abstract nouns (as in 'miser**y**', 'povert**y**'), and -ment and −ness (as in 'excite**ment**, rich**ness**'). Morphemes are useful because, first, they are often consistently spelled (i.e. there are few exceptions), and second, they can be taught as rules for children to remember. For instance, one morpheme rule would be: we spell the 'un' sound ending in words that refer to people as '**ian**' (e.g. 'magic**ian**'), whereas we spell the 'un' ending in abstract words as '**ion**' (e.g. 'situat**ion**'). What I am doing here is making a case for spelling not being about spelling specific words but about learning spelling **patterns** and applying spelling **rules**.

LET'S RECAP

- Most dyslexic children need phonological awareness training alongside learning the alphabet letters and phonic decoding skills.
- Dyslexic children need frequent reading practice to

consolidate their insecure sound-to-letter mappings and to increase their reading speed.
- Phonics helps dyslexic children's spelling but they also need to learn about larger units within words through the teaching of analogy and morphemes.

How we teach children with reading comprehension difficulties

Recall that children with specific reading comprehension difficulties are those who read accurately (and often fluently too) but who cannot understand and remember what they have read. These children almost invariably have underlying oral language difficulties so although they can read words in text accurately, they don't always know what they mean and they find it hard to follow and remember the content of the text. What I will do here is to describe a reading comprehension teaching programme that was developed from a research study carried out by Paula Clarke and her colleagues (2010). They wanted to know whether children's reading comprehension was most improved through oral language teaching or through text (or book level) teaching or indeed through a combination of the two – that is, both oral language and text teaching. What they found was that both types of teaching are needed, and that the single most important teaching aspect involves developing and extending children's vocabulary knowledge.

Let me briefly describe some of the teaching methods they used, beginning with the **oral language programme** which consisted of, for instance:

- **listening activities** such as getting the child to repeat sentences back and having them follow instructions
- **vocabulary enrichment**, which involved introducing the child to a new word, asking them to repeat it, defining it for them and then giving them the opportunity to use the word in a wide range of different contexts and situations

- **oral narrative**, in which the child told stories based around, for example, a sequence of pictures.
- **independent speaking**, in which the child talked about aspects of a book, and engaged in group-based 'show and tell' and 'guess what I'm describing' activities.

The **text level programme** contained teaching strategies such as:

- reading and then **re-reading** the text (mainly used for factual information)
- **highlighting key words** (with a marker pen) and then re-reading the highlighted words to aid memory
- finding difficult words in a passage and looking for clues in the text to work out their **meanings**
- stopping from time to time to **ask questions, think about and discuss** what has been read (**comprehension monitoring**)
- using mental imagery (**a mind picture**) of the text content to support memory
- learning how to make **inferences** by asking questions such as, 'What will happen if...?', 'What could happen next in this story?'
- **thinking out loud** as a strategy for keeping track of what is being read
- explaining and **summarizing** the main point of the passage.

Paula Clarke and her colleagues (2014) have written a book, *Developing Reading Comprehension*, which describes how teachers can use the methods described above in the classroom with children who need extra help with oral language and reading comprehension. Very importantly, the oral language and text comprehension programmes in this study were delivered by teaching assistants, so making it cost effective from the school's point of view. Indeed, teaching assistants can be a valuable resource, not just in terms of reinforcing basic literacy skills, listening to children read and practising key word spellings, but even (as this research study clearly demonstrates) in delivering highly specific and effective teaching programmes.

LET'S RECAP

- Children with poor reading comprehension need teaching programmes that provide instruction in oral language skills (especially vocabulary), as well as developing text-level comprehension strategies.

Is auditory working memory trainable?

As we saw earlier in the book, many children with literacy and language problems show weaknesses in their auditory working memory. It is therefore tempting to ask: would training working memory skills lead to improvements in literacy and language? Professor Susan Gathercole has suggested that working memory is strongly related to learning. Children with working memory difficulties may fail to follow and to remember instructions, they tend to have more limited spoken vocabularies, they struggle with activities that combine processing and storing information (such as mental arithmetic), they have difficulty in place keeping and are error prone, and they may often be mislabelled as having attention problems because they fail to respond to (or more accurately remember) instructions.

Gathercole and Packiam-Alloway (2008), in their very practical book for parents and teachers, have suggested that there are accommodations and strategies that can be set in place to support the child with a weak auditory working memory in both school and home contexts:

- Reducing working memory loads – this can be done by limiting the amount of presented material (e.g. shortening sentences and using accompanying actions to make verbal content more memorable); reducing processing demands by, for instance, simplifying the grammar in instructions; and restructuring complex tasks by breaking them into small, simple steps or by guiding the child through the task using verbal or visual prompts.

- Encouraging the child to request repetition when they need it.
- Supplying memory aids, which might include writing aids (such as spelling flashcards, reminders of how a sentence is structured), mathematics aids (such as number lines, multiplication grids, calculators), audio devices (such as tape recorders that can be replayed for reinforcement) and computer software (such as digital notepads). For these aids to be effective, children need teacher and/or parent instruction, practice and encouragement to use them.
- Developing the child's own use of strategies, such as requesting help from a nominated person, rehearsing verbal information (initially out loud and eventually under their breath), developing a personalized and abbreviated note-taking style, using memory aides like 'chunking' of information, using headings, prompts, diagrams and bullet point lists and so on.

There has been enormous interest of late in computer-based programs which claim to train working memory, in particular *Cogmed* (www.cogmed.com)and *Jungle Memory*™. These programs consist of graded tasks of visual spatial and auditory working memory that are conducted repeatedly over many sessions. The authors of *Cogmed* claim that working through these activities eventually results in benefits to the child's educational attainments, language skills, attention and even IQ. Melby-Lervag and Hulme (2013) reviewed the results of a large number of *Cogmed* and *Jungle Memory* intervention studies. They found that most of the programs led to short-term improvements in working memory but these were not sustained long-term. Even more seriously, positive results were found for only those skills that were close in content to the trained tasks, but there was no evidence of transfer to tasks that were less directly related. This means that working memory training does not easily generalize to targeted skills such as reading and spelling.

Teaching written narrative

As children move from primary to secondary school, there is much more emphasis in the classroom on them being able to express themselves well in written form (i.e. **written narrative**), and also on developing improved higher order skills that are important to exam taking success (i.e. **study and organization skills**).

Karen Harris and her colleagues (2008) in the US have developed a structured and systematic teaching programme to improve students' **written narrative skills**. To be an effective writer, the student needs to be able to:

- decide what they are going to write about
- create an organizational structure by dividing topics into paragraphs; a written plan helps with this, whether it is in the form of a mind map/spider diagram or as a series of bullet points (see the next chapter for how this is done)
- develop arguments and themes and draw conclusions
- proofread to correct spelling and punctuation errors.

Teachers can help children develop these skills through modelling of 'how to do it', discussion of strategies, encouraging the student to think out loud as they work through steps and to memorize through repetition, and giving assistance and feedback.

Teaching study and organization skills

Study and organization skills are about acquiring, recording, organizing, synthesizing, remembering and using information and ideas learned in school. While these skills come naturally to many students, dyslexic children and those with other specific learning difficulties find them a real challenge. However, there is no doubt that these skills, which are so important to higher-level studies, are teachable.

Topics that should be included in teaching children study and organ-ization skills include carrying out research, using the library, doing homework efficiently, studying for exams, and exam technique.

What about alternative therapies?

Alternative therapies receive a lot of attention in the press but parents and teachers need to be aware that they are controversial and that the scientific evidence for their claimed effectiveness is very limited. The logic of these therapies is that a higher-level learning disorder (e.g. of reading or language) is caused by a lower-level biological deficit, most usually at the sensory or motor level. The rationale is that treating the lower-level biological deficit will eventually 'filter through' to the higher cognitive/educational function, thus remediating it. Many of these interventions claim to be grounded in neuroscience research which makes them appear very seductive.

We will look briefly at three types of alternative intervention: tinted lenses, which aim to remediate a reading difficulty at the visual perceptual level; Fast ForWord, a computer-based programme that claims to improve the child's reading and language skills through auditory perception training; and primitive motor reflex resolution, which is a motor-based training method.

The use of **tinted lenses** (or coloured overlays for printed text) was developed by Helen Irlen, who claimed that some poor readers suffer from 'scotopic sensitivity', now more usually referred to as 'visual stress'. This describes the uncomfortable glare and distortion effect which some individuals experience when confronted by black print on a white page. Great claims have been made in the popular press for the instant curative effect of coloured lenses (although these are largely based on anecdotes). However, independent research studies have failed to provide support for the use of tinted lenses in improving reading skill. It has been suggested that coloured lenses might have a role to play alongside systematic teaching in the management of some dyslexic children who appear to experience visual stress. However, in my own clinical experience, I find that many children initially show great enthusiasm for their tinted lenses but this does tend to wane quite quickly, and the lenses are often eventually abandoned. This implies that the lenses have little more than an initial novelty value and ultimately fail to be useful in the medium to long term.

Fast ForWord (www.fastforword.com) is a computer-based intervention programme based on the theory that children with language and literacy difficulties show slow speeds of auditory processing. It consists of a set of computer games that are claimed to improve language and literacy skills by improving the child's auditory processing speed. However, some recent independent studies have shown that Fast ForWord is no more effective in treating literacy and language difficulties than any other treatment (Strong *et al.*, 2011).

A motor-based therapy, **primitive reflex therapy**, draws on a neurological theory that states that children with learning difficulties have failed to replace their early primitive reflexes (like the Moro or palmar reflexes, seen in babies) with more mature postural reflexes. It is proposed that these primitive reflexes need to be revisited before the child can 'move on' in their learning. What this means is that the reflexes need to be replicated (or practised) so that eventually they disappear and, as they do, the child's reading improves. I would suggest that it is highly unlikely that learning to read has anything to do with motor reflexes. Moreover, what research studies have been done have failed to compare children who received the reflex therapy with those in a control group who did not have the therapy.

Biological therapies suffer from a number of general criticisms. First, their claimed effectiveness is largely based on anecdotes or testimonials taken from so-called satisfied parents or clients who have 'witnessed great improvements' in their child's learning. Anecdotes are fine as a means of illustration but they do not constitute proof. The only way to prove that a treatment works is through the carrying out of carefully controlled research trials; unfortunately, these are sadly lacking in the case of biological therapies and the few that have been conducted are rife with problems, such as not using a control group or using the wrong statistics to analyse the results. A further problem for biological therapies is that even if improvements are observed at the sensory/motor levels (which is sometimes the case), these don't seem to 'carry over' to gains in reading or language. Moreover, a number of biological approaches have been criticized because independent researchers have been unable to replicate the results claimed by the proponents of these biological theories; this has certainly been the case for tinted lenses and Fast ForWord. Finally, there is the issue of 'value for money'. The theoretically sound and well-validated phonological training package Sound Linkage costs around £50, while heavily criticized programs such as Fast ForWord can cost upwards of £2000.

LET'S RECAP

- The treatments and interventions described in this chapter are summarized in Box 8.1.

Box 8.1: Literacy difficulties
What to do when the child presents with the following difficulties:

Phonological processing difficulties: Exercises that **train phonological awareness skills** such as blending and segmenting sounds in spoken words are needed (e.g. Sound Linkage).

Auditory working memory difficulties: Computer-based programmes such as *Cogmed* have been met with criticisms. Strategies for adapting the child's learning environment and emphasizing the importance of **reducing memory load** and providing opportunities for **practice and reinforcement** may be more effective.

Decoding difficulties: Systematic **phonics-based** programmes delivered within a structured **multisensory** teaching framework are recommended.

Reading speed/fluency difficulties: Encouraging **regular reading practice** is vital, though more specific strategies such as **repeated reading intervention** may also be used.

Spelling difficulties: Phonics-based spelling programmes that emphasize learning about spelling-to-sound correspondences are recommended initially, although as children reach more advanced levels of spelling additional approaches such as teaching by **analogy** and through **morphemes** are helpful.

Oral language difficulties: Recommended interventions include **vocabulary enrichment**, and **improving listening skills** and **oral narrative**.

Reading comprehension difficulties: The critical components of a reading comprehension intervention programme are **vocabulary enrichment**, teaching what we sometimes call **metacognitive strategies** (e.g. re-reading, mental imagery and comprehension monitoring, reflecting and summarizing) and **inferencing from text**.

Written narrative difficulties: When teaching older children, it is important to support them by encouraging them to adopt **planning strategies** (like using spider diagrams or bullet point lists) to help them better structure and organize their written output.

A cautionary note: The evidence for biological-based therapies such as tinted lenses, auditory training and reflex therapy is very limited; while seemingly attractive, these have limited theoretical validity, have not been subjected to rigorous scientific treatment trials and are often very expensive.

In this chapter and in Chapter 10, our case studies will be revisited to provide examples of intervention planning, specific recommendations needed to target each child's individual problems and a comment on likely future outcome. The first case study for intervention is that of Alex, our 12-year-old with severe dyslexia occurring in the context of a developmental language disorder.

CASE STUDY 1: ALEX, WHO HAS SEVERE DYSLEXIA AND ORAL LANGUAGE DIFFICULTIES

Alex's intervention plan

Alex has very severe dyslexia with co-occurring milder (and improving) oral language difficulties, both of which need to be addressed so that his educational needs can be met over the remaining years of his secondary schooling. Regular and frequent one-to-one instruction in literacy needs to be integrated with interventions that target his vocabulary knowledge, oral and reading comprehension and written narrative. Accommodations in the classroom and for exams, together with some subject differentiation, will also be required to ensure that he is able to access his curriculum.

Specific recommendations

- Provision of a structured phonological/phonics literacy intervention that targets phonological awareness, phonic decoding and spelling rules (within a flexible, multisensory teaching framework that includes real book experience).
- Provision of an integrated language and reading comprehension programme that develops oral vocabulary and higher order language skills, together with text-based strategies such as re-reading and highlighting key points, questioning and summarizing.
- Encouragement to take advantage of voice-activated, editing and spellcheck facilities that technology offers, while being allowed to submit a significant proportion of course work in word-processed form.
- Being permitted time accommodations, access to a reader and either provision of a scribe or use of a laptop computer in written examinations.
- Provision of curricula and classroom accommodations, such as exemption from taking a foreign language, use of photocopied notes and access to a mentor who can support the development of improved study and organizational skills.

- Ensuring that Alex is not overloaded with too many subjects at GCSE, and encouraging him to select subjects that capitalize on his relative strength in maths and his good non-verbal skills (art, design and technology).

Future progress and outcome

Alex's outcome will, of course, be impacted by his very severe dyslexia, occurring in the context of earlier marked language delay. While this might lead us to predict a generally poor long-term outcome for Alex, we need to bear in mind that he has a significant number of **positive moderators** (or factors) that would be expected to improve his outcome. These include early identification and intensive intervention for his language disorder, having good non-verbal skills which might provide some compensatory resources and which contribute to his stronger maths ability, a supportive home environment and good levels of psychological adjustment and motivation. With continued targeted intervention, curricula and examination accommodations, access to technology and high levels of teacher and parent support, it should be possible for Alex to obtain school-based qualifications and to then proceed to further education courses which reflect his relative strengths within the non-verbal and mathematical domains of ability.

I'll conclude this chapter by describing the intervention plan and programme for Susanna, our second language learner, whose assessment was described in the previous chapter.

● SUSANNA, A SECOND LANGUAGE LEARNER WHO IS STRUGGLING IN BOTH ORAL AND WRITTEN ENGLISH

Susanna's intervention plan

Susanna needs to continue with EAL (English as an additional language) and targeted literacy support. Additionally, it will be advisable to seek further assessment of her language skills by a speech and language therapist.

Specific recommendations

- Referral to a speech and language therapist for a more detailed evaluation of Susanna's language skills in English; face-to-face therapy may be indicated but the therapist should also recommend programmes that can be used at home and school that improve her vocabulary and grammar.
- Susanna should continue with a systematic literacy programme that includes phonological awareness training, phonic decoding and learning about spelling-to-sound rules, delivered within a structured multisensory framework.
- Susanna's reading comprehension should improve as her oral English develops, although some specific teaching of reading comprehension strategies may be needed.
- Susanna's parents need to encourage her to read English books and watch English TV and videos (especially during lengthy holidays likely to be spent in France), to ensure that she has sufficient exposure to English oral and print environments.
- Susanna may need teaching assistant support from time to time in the classroom so that she can cope with the comprehension demands placed on her in an oral instruction environment.

KEY MESSAGES TO TAKE AWAY

✓ Children with word-level reading difficulties (dyslexia) need phonological awareness and letter knowledge training before they are ready for a systematic phonics programme that teaches them about spelling-to-sound correspondences.

✓ Reading practice is the key to increasing reading speed and fluency; a teaching strategy called repeated reading intervention has been shown to lead to improvements in reading speed (and even comprehension).

✓ Dyslexic poor spellers need teaching strategies that

go beyond learning about simple sound-to-letter correspondences; they need to learn about analogies (word families) and morphemes (units of meaning) that are more reliably and consistently spelled.

✓ Dyslexic children who have co-occurring language difficulties and those with reading comprehension problems need teaching methods that improve their comprehension, narrative and, in particular, vocabulary skills – at both the oral language and written text levels.

✓ Biological interventions that target skills at the perceptual and motor levels should be approached with caution, as most are based on theories that are not well validated and have not been subjected to scientifically controlled studies that demonstrate that they really do work.

Chapter 9

Supporting the Child with Literacy Difficulties in the Classroom

In this chapter I describe how:

→ it is possible to incorporate components of specialist literacy intervention programmes within the classroom learning context

→ research has shown that teaching assistants (and also potentially classroom volunteers and parents) can be a valuable resource, not only in practising and reinforcing children's learning but even in delivering selected special teaching programmes

→ you, as a class teacher, can improve your dyslexic pupil's reading accuracy and their speed of reading simply through regular practice and reinforcement

→ spelling can be improved through teaching methods that enable 'overlearning' of common (high-frequency) key words and curriculum-based words, and through encouraging proofreading and the use of dictionaries and computer spellcheckers

→ working on your pupil's vocabulary knowledge, oral narrative, listening comprehension and oral expression not only improves their understanding in the classroom, but is also key to developing good reading comprehension

→ you can support your pupil's written narrative and their study and organization abilities, skills that are so important to success at secondary school

→ you can build and maintain your pupil's motivation to learn.

In the previous chapter, I described the teaching methods that have been demonstrated to be effective in teaching children with literacy difficulties. Of course, all children, as part of the National Literacy Strategy, receive teaching in phonological skills, phonics, spelling, comprehension and writing. But children with literacy difficulties, while no doubt benefiting from this, are likely to require additional specialist interventions – and certainly more practice and reinforcement than the typical learner.

In this chapter, I re-work the teaching components described in Chapter 8 in a way that is adaptable to the classroom (and occasionally the home context). As part of a pupil's Individual Educational Plan (IEP), the child with a literacy difficulty may well have 'pull out' one-to-one or group-based intervention sessions with the SENCo or a specialist literacy teacher. Classroom teachers do of course have their hands full delivering the National Literacy Strategy to all their pupils – so they have limited capacity to devote extra time to the individual child who has a literacy difficulty. However, with advice and support from the SENCo or from specialist assessors, it is possible to incorporate some of the components of these intervention programmes into the classroom context. As pointed out in the previous chapter, there have been scientific studies that have clearly demonstrated that trained and supported teaching assistants can deliver specific interventions, as well as provide much-needed opportunities for practice and reinforcement of key literacy skills. And there is no reason why teachers cannot also draw on the willingness and enthusiasm of classroom volunteers and many parents to work with individual children to support their progress in reading, writing and spelling.

Supporting reading and spelling skills
Training phonological skills
The phonological exercises described earlier in the previous chapter and the Sound Linkage programme that was recommended are designed to be delivered mainly by specialist teachers. While some phonological awareness exercises may be incorporated into shared 'on the carpet' activities in Reception and Year 1, children who have dyslexia will almost certainly need a more individualized and

172

structured phonological programme (like Sound Linkage) that is delivered one-to-one – and usually beyond the first two years at school. A phonological programme designed with classroom teachers, teaching assistants and even parents in mind is *My Special Alphabet Book*, which I wrote with my colleague Dr Helen Likierman (2022). This is geared towards working with young children who are proving slow to learn to read, including children whose oral language is delayed. It is designed for both parents and teachers to use, and we do feel that it is classroom teacher/teaching assistant- and parent-friendly. It begins with teaching the child the alphabet letters and sounds in the context of a story about 'saving the environment'. It then goes on to describe phonological awareness training exercises in some detail. An important point to bear in mind is that if phonological awareness training is to be conducted by teaching assistants, classroom volunteers or parents, it is important that they pronounce the speech sounds correctly; a good guide to correct pronunciation can be found at www.youtube.com/watch?v=-ksblMiliA8. *My Special Alphabet Book* also describes phonological linkage activities in the context of introducing the child to the beginning stages of phonic decoding.

Teaching phonic decoding skills

Systematic phonics is the recommended core teaching method for all children in the early stages of learning to read, though children with dyslexia are likely to require more intensive one-to-one or group-based decoding instruction than the typical learner. There is a huge range of phonics-based teaching programmes that work well for dyslexic children; these include Alpha to Omega, Jolly Phonics, Toe by Toe (which is teaching assistant- and even parent-friendly), Phono-Graphix, and Kelly and Phillips' (2022) *Teaching Literacy to Learners with Dyslexia*. Which phonics programme is chosen for the class in general and for dyslexic children in particular is to some degree a matter of teacher choice and preference, though an aid to selecting the programmes most suitable for children with literacy difficulties is Brook's (2016) *What Works Best For Children And Young People With Literacy Difficulties?* Practising (and so overlearning) sound-to-letter correspondences so they become automatised is an activity that can be carried out by teaching assistants, classroom volunteers and sometimes by parents.

173

Involving parents in reading practice

No person in a child's life has more time and opportunity to practise reading skills with them than their parent. Arguably, listening to their child read out loud at home on a frequent and regular basis is the single most important thing a parent can do to support their child's reading development. Reading out loud gives children the opportunity to practise their decoding skills, to expand their word-specific reading vocabulary, to become familiar with common words and to increase their reading speed and fluency. As a classroom teacher, it is hugely helpful if you can encourage the parent of a child with literacy difficulties to spend 10–15 minutes most days of the week listening to their child read – using reading materials geared to their child's current reading level and with content that is in line with their interests. You will be able to guide them as to their child's reading level and also be able to suggest suitable books they can read together at home. I usually advise the parent to encourage their child to 'sound out' words they do not instantly recognize, but to help them if they get really stuck. And of course, they need to talk about the content of what they are reading – the main purpose of reading is for meaning and for pleasure too. If their child is a reluctant reader, you might suggest that they 'take turns' in reading the story, or they could use a reward scheme to help keep up their child's interest and motivation.

Examples of home-based **rewards for 'reading willingly'** could include:

- on finishing the reading session, letting the child watch a favourite TV programme or play a chosen computer game
- using a star or sticker chart where the child earns a sticker for 'working hard on their reading' and then exchanges a certain number of accumulated stickers for a larger reward (which could be a favourite pudding, time on a computer game, a weekend outing of their choice, a small toy and so on)
- using a points system which works much like a sticker or star chart but is a bit more sophisticated and will

appeal to older children (to earn pocket money and more grown-up rewards).

★ Increasing reading speed

In the last chapter I talked about **repeated reading intervention** as the teaching method that has been shown to be most effective in increasing children's reading speed. This is a technique that teaching assistants, classroom volunteers or parents at home can fairly easily employ. It is really an extension of reading practice but is conducted slightly differently. These are the steps that need to be followed:

- The adult chooses a reading passage of say half- to three-quarters of a page in length that is at the child's reading level.
- They then ask the child to read the passage out loud over and over again until they achieve a faster speed.
- The adult will need to time the child's reading speed using a stopwatch or timer and to plot it on a chart or graph. This will enable them to keep track of the increases in the child's reading speed and also importantly provide them with feedback of their increasing speed (which can help to keep up their motivation).
- When the graph or chart shows that the child is reading at a faster speed and with more fluency, they need to move on to a different parallel passage and read that over and over again.

Some important points to bear in mind about repeated reading intervention:

- The sessions need to be kept short (no longer than ten minutes), and conducted at least five times per week.
- The repeated reading sessions should continue over a period of at least three or four months before significant improvements in the child's reading speed can be expected.
- Because this is a repetitive and for many children a rather boring activity, it is very likely that a reward scheme will

need to be used (of the sort described in the previous section).

- Children may need 'breaks away' from repeated reading intervention, especially if they are showing signs of resistance.

Teaching spelling

Spelling is a long-term problem for most dyslexic individuals, even those who eventually learn to read reasonably well. The child's learning of phonics will help them develop knowledge of spelling patterns – but only up to a point. There is now more emphasis on children learning larger units within words, like analogies and morphemes which are more consistently spelled (see the previous chapter). While teaching larger units is incorporated to some degree within the National Literacy Strategy, most children with dyslexia will need their awareness and use of these to be integrated alongside phonics into a specific (individually tailored) spelling programme (although it is possible to practise and reinforce specific rimes and morphemes within the classroom context and through sent-home spelling lists).

★ WORKING ON KEY WORD SPELLINGS

The Oxford English Corpus lists the 100 most common words in the English language. These 100 words together make up 50 per cent of all the words we read and write – all children need to know how to spell these correctly. Unfortunately, many of them are irregularly spelled so phonics isn't much help here. Dyslexic children find learning key words challenging and they make errors on the same words over and over again – even after they have encountered them multiple times during their reading and writing experiences. Yet again, teaching assistants, classroom volunteers and parents can be a valuable resource in practising key word spellings.

The 100 most common words are listed in Box 9.1 below. The first 12 make up one quarter of the words we read and write so these need to be learned first. The next 20 words make up one third of all the words we read and write and so these should be learned next. And the remainder should be learned last of all.

Box 9.1: The commonest words in the English language

a	and	he	I	in	is
it	of	that	the	to	was

all	are	as	at	be	but
for	had	have	him	his	not
on	one	said	so	they	we
with	you				

about	an	back	been	before	big
by	call	came	can	come	could
did	do	down	first	from	get
go	has	her	here	if	into
just	like	little	look	made	make
me	more	much	must	my	new
no	now	off	old	only	or
other	our	out	over	right	see
she	some	their	them	then	there
this	two	up	want	well	went
were	what	when	where	which	who
will	your				

HOW TO TEACH KEY WORD SPELLINGS

The general consensus is that the best way to learn key word spellings is through **Simultaneous Oral Spelling (SOS)**. Here are the steps:

- Show the child the written key word and ask them to remember it.

- Then cover it with your hand or a piece of paper and ask the child to write the word from memory – while saying the name (not the sound) of each letter as they write it (i.e. 'zed' not 'zzz', 'kay' not 'k').
- Remove the covering and check if the word is written correctly.
- Repeat this process until the child has spelled the word correctly at least three times.
- Keep going back to these spellings from time to time to make sure that the child has remembered them.

LOOKING FOR SPELLING PATTERNS

The Simultaneous Oral Spelling method can be used for any new word a child is learning to spell, not just key words but also words from spelling lists that are employed within the classroom and which may be sent home from school. Spelling lists usually emphasize a particular pattern – for instance, words with 'ight' endings or words containing the grapheme 'ee'. It is helpful to point out these spelling patterns to the child so that they can become aware of them and indeed look out for them when they see them in words they read or are asked to spell.

★ LEARNING CURRICULA SPECIFIC SPELLINGS

When older children encounter subjects like geography, history or the sciences, they will be introduced to a special, often technical, vocabulary that is specific to that subject. So they see the same spellings over and over again in the curriculum books they are set – words like 'temperature', 'electricity' and so on. It is a good idea to make a list of these curricula-specific spellings for each subject so that the child has them to hand and becomes increasingly familiar with them. The Simultaneous Oral Spelling approach can be used to teach the words until they are overlearned.

PROOFREADING FOR SPELLING ERRORS

Many children with dyslexia will rush through a piece of written work, with the result that it is peppered with spelling errors. Often, however, with re-reading and checking, at least some of these spelling errors can be detected and corrected – thus reducing the child's spelling error rate (and helping them earn a better mark for their written effort). Older children in particular should be encouraged to proofread their written work. One way to do this is to mark in the margin of each line of writing whether or not there are spelling (and perhaps also punctuation) errors, and how many of each there are. So for instance, writing '2 SPs' and '1 P' in the margin next to the line would indicate to the child that there are two spelling errors and one punctuation error in that line. This margin prompting draws the child's attention to existing errors and the adult can then help them find and correct these. As the child becomes more proficient in this, adult assistance and the margin prompts can be gradually withdrawn.

USING DICTIONARIES AND SPELLCHECKERS

Dictionaries have of course been used for centuries to help people learn how to spell and in particular to check if their spellings are correct. Using a conventional dictionary is hard for dyslexic individuals but there are some that are specially designed for the dyslexic student. The best known is the *ACE Spelling Dictionary* (Moseley and Nicol, 1995). This is suitable for the older student who has at least a basic spelling vocabulary. The *ACE Spelling Dictionary* works well because the vowel sounds are coded as they sound, as opposed to their visual spelling patterns – so making it much more user-friendly for the dyslexic child for whom 'seeing' spelling patterns is a challenge. Teachers and parents need to support the child for quite a long time before they get the hang of using the *ACE Spelling Dictionary*.

It is also a good idea for children to build up their own **personalized spelling dictionary.** To do this, they need either an exercise book divided into the 26 letters of the alphabet or a set of separate flash cards arranged alphabetically in a box. Each word the child is finding hard to learn to spell is written on a separate page or flashcard, along with a short and simple definition of its meaning (and maybe for younger children a cut-out picture or drawing which exemplifies the word and its meaning). The Simultaneous Oral Spelling method of teaching can be used to teach the spelling of the word. The words in the dictionary need to be revisited from time to time to ensure that the child has not forgotten them.

Of course, realistically these days, most poor spellers draw on technology to help them spell words correctly. As children proceed through the latter stages of primary school and on into their secondary school years, they will use computers more and hand in their projects, essays and homework in word-processed form. This means, of course, that they can make use of the **spellcheck**. Early on, many dyslexic children need guidance and support from teachers and parents to use the spellcheck correctly, but with practice it can prove an enormous technological aid, especially at secondary school.

COMPUTER READING AND SPELLING PROGRAMS AND GAMES
Literacy-based computer games can be used to help back up and reinforce face-to-face teaching of reading and spelling. These can be readily used both in the classroom context and at home and are often very appealing to dyslexic children who may be easily 'turned off' by traditional paper-based reading and writing materials. For instance, *Wordshark* consists of a series of graded computer activities (linked to the dyslexia teaching package Alpha to Omega) which teach and reinforce the learning of sound-to-letter correspondences. It is especially engaging for children because it looks to them like a computer 'game' (sharks swim across the screen gobbling up letters). Another recommended programme is *Touch-type Read and Spell*, which is a computerized scheme where children learn spelling patterns alongside developing touch-typing skills. *Nessy Fingers* can also be used for teaching touch-typing and keyboarding skills to children aged seven and upwards.

LET'S RECAP

- Class teachers can support the dyslexic reader by reinforcing phonological and phonic learning and through strongly emphasizing regular reading practice.
- Repeated reading intervention (reading the same text over and over again) is a proven method of increasing reading speed.
- Simultaneous Oral Spelling (say-cover-write-check) is

> helpful for learning new words, especially irregularly
> spelled key words.
> – Proofreading techniques, special dictionaries, literacy-
>   based computer games and spellchecks can help
>   improve dyslexic children's spelling accuracy.
> – Classroom assistants, volunteers and parents provide
>   an invaluable resource for reinforcing and practising
>   children's reading and spelling skills.

Supporting reading comprehension skills

In the previous chapter, we saw how helping children with reading comprehension difficulties needs to focus on improving oral
language skills alongside text level comprehension. Some children
who struggle with reading comprehension have marked underlying
oral language difficulties that may require an assessment by a
speech and language therapist and even a course of speech and
language therapy. If a pupil does have weak oral language skills,
it will be important to talk through with the SENCo how they can
be best helped at school – and whether a programme such as the
one described in the previous chapter could be used.

What could be done within the classroom to help the pupil with
reading comprehension difficulties? In the research study conducted by Paula Clarke and her colleagues (2010) described in the
last chapter, the oral language and text comprehension instruction that proved so effective in developing the children's reading
comprehension was delivered by trained and supervised teaching
assistants. These methods are described in more detail below and
are possible for class teachers to integrate into the school day,
in group-based sessions and with the involvement of teaching
assistants or classroom volunteers.

Oral language

Four key areas to work on here are vocabulary, oral narrative, listening comprehension and oral expression.

VOCABULARY

There is a lot of evidence to show that children with reading comprehension difficulties have a limited vocabulary – that is, they don't know the meanings of words they read and so find it difficult to follow the text. When you read with a pupil and you come across words you think they might not know, ask them to tell you what they mean. If they can't, this could be the starting point for building up a personalized dictionary (or bank) of words and their meanings. As with spelling, use an exercise book; write the word at the top of the page followed by a simple and easily remembered definition and maybe even a picture or drawing to exemplify its meaning. You and the child will need to regularly revisit the words in the dictionary to make sure that they are remembering and retaining them. If you feel that you want to look at what is called **vocabulary enrichment** in more depth, the excellent book *Bringing Words to Life: Robust Vocabulary Instruction*, by Isabel Beck and her colleagues (2002), is very user-friendly and practical.

★ ORAL NARRATIVE

Here is an example of a method to help your pupil develop **storytelling skills** – one of the key aspects of both oral narrative and reading comprehension.

Have a set of pictures of people, places, things and so on, each of which should fall into one of four categories: **who** (pictures of people), **where** (places), **when** and **what** (events and happenings). Say to the child, 'We are going to make up a story using our story cards. First, we decide **who** our story is about, then we have to decide **where** our story takes place; after that we decide **when** it takes place and finally **what** happens in the story.' A picture is used for each of the four categories and the child then makes up a sentence for each: for example, 'There was a little girl called Leila [**who**]. She lived in a house in a village called Frumpley [**where**]. It was the summer holidays and Leila was off school [**when**]. Leila went on a special trip with her grandparents on a steam train... [**what**].' You then need to ask what might happen next and eventually how the story ends. It can sometimes be helpful to get the younger child to act out the story.

Teaching **story structure** helps children to understand logical sequences such as beginning, middle, end, high point (or climax), resolutions and so on. Story planners (perhaps using prompt flash-cards) can be useful to mark the:

- **beginning or setting** – characters, time and place
- **middle** – what happens, action, reaction
- **end** – result and message.

For young children, the structure of the story can be explained in a diagram – for instance using a **story mountain**, which shows how a story is built up, working through the stages from an 'opening', through a 'build up' to a 'problem', then climaxing in an 'event' that solves the problem and finishing with a 'resolution' that leads to an 'ending'.

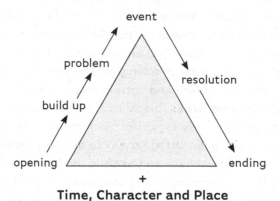

Time, Character and Place

Figure 9.1: The story mountain

And then there is **independent speaking**, where you ask the child to talk about aspects of a book they have read, or engage in 'show and tell' and 'guess what I'm describing' activities.

LISTENING COMPREHENSION

Children are not able to understand what they read until they can understand what they hear. So before you work on text reading comprehension, it is a good idea to do some listening comprehension exercises. Read a passage out loud to your pupil, asking them to listen carefully and to remember what is being read. You can then either ask the child to recall what they have heard or you could ask them specific questions about the content. You will need to start with short and simple passages and then gradually move towards longer and more complicated passages.

ORAL EXPRESSION

There are some day-to-day techniques that speech and language therapists recommend for helping young children improve how they express themselves orally:

- **Expand and recast:** This can be used when the child says a short sentence that has missing words or incorrect vocabulary or grammar. You repeat what they have said back to them in a longer and expanded version, with better vocabulary and, if necessary, corrected grammar. For example, the child says, 'I drawed a picture with a dog.' You respond, 'You drew a picture of a dog; let's draw some other things in your picture like a kennel, a dog bowl and a bone.' What you are doing here is expanding what they have said into a lengthier sentence with more interesting vocabulary and corrected grammar.
- **Reflect and reinforce:** This is useful when the child tends to produce only very short sentences or phrases that you want to encourage them to build on. You say the sentence or phrase back to the child (reflect) and then expand it with comments and questions that help develop a conversation (reinforce). For instance, the child might say, 'I drew a picture of a dog.' You say, 'You drew a picture of a dog. That sounds interesting. What sort of dog was it and what was it doing?'

For further ideas on how to improve young children's oral language, have a look at the relevant sections in *My Special Alphabet Book* (Muter and Likierman, 2022).

The **Nuffield Early Language Intervention (NELI)** is a highly recommended commercially available programme that is designed for use with young children who have poor oral language skills and for those at risk of developing related reading difficulties. The intervention consists of a 20-week withdrawal programme that is delivered in the Reception year; there are three 30-minute group and two 15-minute individual sessions per week that cover oral narrative, listening skills, vocabulary and, later on, letter knowledge and phonological awareness. The programme is highly prescriptive and consequently can be delivered by teaching assistants under the supervision of a class teacher or SENCo. Scientifically conducted studies have shown that NELI has to date benefited nearly 6000 children, with big gains in the children's oral language (including for socially disadvantaged children and EAL (English as an Additional Language) learners), with smaller gains for reading and behaviour.

Reading comprehension

Here are some tips for working on children's reading comprehension:

- Check the child's **text reading comprehension** – ask them to read a story to you and then get them to summarize it and tell it back to you or ask them questions about what they have read.
- If the child finds this reading comprehension check difficult, try these tips to help:
  - Get the child to re-read the passage (just going over something more than once helps understanding and recall).
  - Get them to 'look back over' the story to find key points.
  - Use clues or questions for finding key points including **Where? Who? When? Why? How? What next? How does it end?**
  - Get them to talk out loud about the key points.
  - Get them to create a picture image of the key point in their mind's eye to help with remembering.
- For older children, it can be helpful to photocopy what the child is to read and then supply them with a coloured highlighter pen. Initially with your guidance, encourage them to read through the passage while highlighting (through asterisking, circling and underlining) the key points in the passage. After the child has done this, they

185

should re-read only the highlighted parts in order to **focus attention** on them, to **rehearse** them (out loud if needed) and so to **consolidate** them in their memory store.

The child then either free recalls the story, or answers questions on it – which can be in oral or written form.

- Help the child develop the skill of **making inferences**. Ask them about what might happen next (where this is not stated) or how a character might be feeling (again when not given). You could also ask the child to supply an alternative ending or ask what they think the outcome might be if something other than the action described in the passage had happened.

LET'S RECAP

- Teaching children who have poor reading comprehension requires interventions that address their underlying oral language difficulties, as well as their text-based weaknesses.
- Oral language teaching needs to target vocabulary, listening comprehension, oral expression and oral narrative.
- Text level programmes should focus on teaching children with poor reading comprehension strategies like re-reading, highlighting and rehearsal of key points, and inference making.

Supporting auditory working memory difficulties

In the previous chapter, there was a list of accommodations and practical strategies that can help support the child who has auditory working memory difficulties (this is based on Gathercole and Packiam Alloway's workbook, 2008). These can be used both at school and at home. Look back at these and see which could be helpful to your pupil. I would advise against buying into computer-based working memory programmes as I have concerns about how well they generalize to targeted skills such as reading and spelling – the child might get better at the computer games with practice, but this may well not 'carry over' to the educational skills you want to improve.

★ Supporting written narrative skills

Writing a piece of text seems to come naturally to many students but for children with literacy difficulties it can be a very real challenge – even after they have shown improvements in their basic reading, writing and spelling skills. These children need guidance in how to write up a project or produce an essay. Components of good written narrative are taught within the National Literacy Strategy, including sentence construction, grammar, punctuation and so on, but many children with literacy difficulties complain that they just don't know how to get started to produce a piece of written narrative. It is important to support them with this. The content of what they write should have been covered in whole class lessons, whether English, history or whatever. But children with literacy difficulties often need help with the **structure** and **organization** of what they produce. Planning is key here. Some students work best with a spider diagram, some with a list of key bullet points, but the principles are much the same. They need to start with a title, and then list in order the key words which signal a separate paragraph for each idea. They then build in additional sentences based around each key word, not forgetting the introduction as the beginning paragraph and the conclusion as the final paragraph.

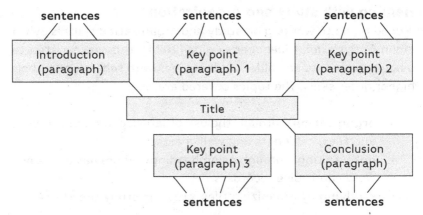

Figure 9.2: A simplified spider diagram

187

A bullet point plan

- Introduction paragraph
  - Sentence 1
  - Sentence 2
- Key point/paragraph 1
  - Sentence 1
  - Sentence 2
  - Sentence 3
- Key point/paragraph 2
  - Sentence 1
  - Sentence 2
  - Sentence 3
- Key point/paragraph 3
  - Sentence 1
  - Sentence 2
  - Sentence 3
  - Sentence 4
- Conclusion paragraph
  - Sentence 1
  - Sentence 2

Using plans like these help children structure their written work and organize it into sequenced and ordered paragraphs – which massively improves the quality of their written output.

Helping with study and organization

A good guide to working on study and organization skills is Sylvia Moody's *Dyslexia: A Teenager's Guide* (2004); this was written to guide adolescents and older students in how to self-improve their higher order skills. The topics covered are:

- **organization**, through the use of labelled stacking trays and files, calendars and wall charts
- **note-taking**, through using headings, abbreviations, key words and voice recorders
- **studying** by organizing files, creating study time tables,

using mind maps and charts, doing verbal rehearsal and talking through topics with a friend or family member

- **taking exams**, including time management, re-reading questions and underlining key words.

Coping with homework

Getting children with literacy difficulties to do their homework can create a lot of stress in families. The child who struggles with reading and writing is often reluctant to settle to homework, and this can easily lead to family conflict and rows. Here are some tips to pass on to parents so that homework is less stressful for all:

- Homework needs to become part of the child's school routine, with a period of time set aside each evening and at weekends.
- Discuss with the pupil's parent how much time is expected to be spent on homework – probably 20–30 minutes daily for primary-age children, 60–90 minutes daily for secondary-age children.
- Homework should begin around 20–30 minutes after arriving home from school, maybe after having a snack but definitely before watching TV or playing computer games.
- Advise parents to start the homework session by making a plan (maybe in the form of a simple chart), listing what topics are to be covered.
- Children who have concentration difficulties and secondary-age children may need a rest break half-way through, perhaps for a snack or a conversational chat (but TV or computer games during the break should be avoided).
- Advise the parent to be on hand to answer questions or support their child generally, and to check with them how it is going.
- Use rewards (star/sticker charts or points systems) for 'staying on task', completing the homework tasks and meeting deadlines.

If your school has the resources to offer a homework club that is supervised by a teaching assistant or older student, this can be recommended to the parent who is trying to avoid homework-based rows at home that can impact negatively their relationship with their child.

★ Motivating the child with a literacy difficulty

Many children with specific learning difficulties experience strong feelings of failure, low self-worth and frustration because (as it seems to them), in spite of their efforts they don't progress as do their classmates. Not surprisingly, they lose the motivation to learn which may present as 'giving up', avoiding work, telling their parents they have no homework, making excuses for not settling to work and so on. Parents and teachers often find themselves expending a lot of effort trying to restore and then maintain the child's lost motivation. Here are some general techniques to engage and motivate the pupil with a literacy difficulty:

- Encourage areas of competence even if these are not academic – sports, art and so on.
- Use praise for 'on-task' behaviour, completing tasks and meeting deadlines – say, 'Well done', 'That's great', 'You tried really hard'.
- Set up a **mentoring system** – for example, a teaching assistant or even an older mature student who meets with the child regularly to provide non-judgemental advice, support, praise and encouragement.
- Set goals in graded, realistic and achievable steps and present work in small manageable 'chunks'.
- Use 'positive language' to describe what the child needs to do (as opposed to criticizing them for not doing it) – saying, 'That's particularly hard, isn't it? Let's try and think of another way of doing it that might be easier' instead of 'Come on, you can do better, try it again.'

A more targeted approached to motivating students which I've touched on before is that of using specific **rewards** or **reinforcers** that are given to the child for being 'on-task' and for completing prescribed activities. Younger children will usually respond to a simple sticker or star chart which is backed by more concrete rewards (negotiated with parents), such as having access to a favourite computer game, earning a small toy, choosing a favourite pudding for dessert or having a special outing. Older children will require a more sophisticated reward programme, such as a points system, which might be sold to them as a form of **performance-related pay**; points can be added up to earn more teenage-appropriate concrete rewards (again negotiated with parents), such as having a sleepover or earning pocket money.

KEY MESSAGES TO TAKE AWAY

✓ By drawing on advice and support from assessors and the SENCo, and capitalizing on the additional teaching resources made possible by assistants, classroom volunteers and parents, class teachers can play an invaluable role in promoting the learning and progress of children with literacy difficulties.

✓ Reading regularly with the child who has literacy difficulties is crucial to reinforcing sound-to-letter knowledge, practising decoding skills, expanding their word-specific vocabulary and increasing speed and fluency – and can be easily delivered by support workers and parents at home.

✓ Reinforcing and practising key word spellings and learning curricula-specific spellings, drawing children's attention to regular spelling patterns and rules, and encouraging the use of personalized dictionaries and technology-based spellchecks can go a long way to increasing the dyslexic child's spelling vocabulary.

✓ Reading for meaning is the main goal of reading – children with reading comprehension difficulties need explicit teaching at the oral language level (vocabulary, oral narrative etc.), together with strategies for developing text-based comprehension.

✓ Supporting the development of the child's written narrative, study and organization skills is important to their success at secondary school when the passing of exams assumes increasing importance.

✓ Advising parents on how to manage homework conflicts and working with them to improve and to maintain the child's motivation are critical to guarantee their engagement with learning.

Chapter 10

How to Support the Child with Co-occurring Difficulties

In this chapter I describe how:

→ children with co-occurring arithmetic difficulties need special teaching that not only systematically builds their number knowledge (from the concrete to the abstract), but also recognizes their need for frequent practice and revision so they consolidate and retain that knowledge
→ children with co-occurring severe ADHD benefit most from medication, but those with milder difficulties can show improvements through restructuring their learning environment (both at home and at school), through good behavioural management and through dietary modifications and supplements
→ children with co-occurring motor coordination difficulties need systematic handwriting instruction in their early school years but are most helped through access to technology (in particular, laptops) in their senior school years.

In the previous two chapters, we looked in detail at methods of teaching children with dyslexia and also those with reading comprehension difficulties – most of which are school-based, although some can be carried out, or at least practised and reinforced, by class teachers and teaching assistants. In this chapter, I deal with how we teach and manage dyslexic children who have a **simultaneous co-occurring difficulty.** Having an additional learning problem does of course complicate the educational picture for a very large number of children. I describe interventions and teaching methods that target these co-occurring difficulties – some of these are school-based, some need clinic settings and some can be done at home by the parents. We look at co-occurring arithmetic, attention and visual motor difficulties in turn and revisit the case studies that exemplify these, showing how both the child's literacy and their co-occurring difficulties are addressed.

Teaching and supporting children with co-occurring specific arithmetic difficulty/dyscalculia

For children with dyslexia and co-occurring dyscalculia, it is as important to recognize, assess and provide special teaching for their arithmetic difficulties as it is for their literacy problems. However, we know far less about teaching children with arithmetic difficulties than we do about teaching children with literacy difficulties.

We saw in earlier chapters that many children with arithmetic difficulties have a deficit of **numerosity** (their understanding of the magnitude of number). We might ask if it is possible to train up numerosity in a child presenting with an arithmetic difficulty. There have been some attempts at developing computer programs that train children to, for example, count dots, with the number of dots increasing in a graded fashion as the child aims to work faster and faster. While a program such as this might result in improvements in dot counting performance, I suspect that we would see little evidence of **transfer** to more general arithmetic skills (the same problem we had with *Cogmed* and other working memory computer programs).

It is probably far more effective to directly remediate the specific number weaknesses experienced by the child with an arithmetic difficulty. The programmes that seem to work best are those that:

- contain explicit instruction in specific maths skills; for example, explaining to the child the concept of fractions, what they mean and how to write and calculate them
- give instruction in general methods for carrying out particular arithmetic operations; for example, the method for doing complex subtraction with pay-back

- teach children to give verbal descriptions – the child is encouraged to talk through arithmetic steps as they carry them out, which plays a reinforcing role
- provide the child with a range of examples related to the specific strategy or method, mainly through backing up and reinforcing with lots of pencil-and-paper worksheet practice.

Some children's arithmetic struggles are caused not by a weakness in numerosity but by visual spatial or working memory difficulties. Children with visual spatial difficulties are likely to have trouble with maths concepts that have a strong visual basis, such as geometry and symmetry, fractions, drawing graphs and understanding time. These children need extra teaching that specifically targets these visually based aspects of their maths curriculum, perhaps encouraging them to develop verbal strategies like 'talking through' the steps or processes involved. For children with working memory difficulties, programmes that build in practice and reinforcement of arithmetic skills and concepts are important: Kumon and related schemes, which strongly emphasize repetition through regular and frequent worksheet practice, can be especially helpful for children whose poor working memory is holding them back.

Examples of specific systematic maths programmes that are used in the UK to support children with maths problems are **Numicon**, **Addacus** and **Dynamo Maths**:

- **Numicon**[1] (2001) follows a sequence of teaching that begins with the child working with **concrete materials.** Flat plastic shapes with holes represent the numbers from 1 to 10, with each number having its own colour. Children use these concrete materials to learn patterns, sequencing, ordering and calculating to solve simple number problems. They then go on to use **visual imagery** with pictures and lastly to develop **abstract maths concepts.** Teacher surveys conducted by Numicon from 2008 to 2011 showed a 47 per cent increase in students

---

1   See https://global.oup.com/education/content/primary/series/numicon/?region=uk.

achieving (above average) Level 3 at Key Stage 1 after using Numicon, and a 72 per cent increase in students achieving (above average) level 5 at Key Stage 2, having used Numicon in Key Stage 1.

- **Addacus**[2] is a numeracy activity pack with photocopiable worksheets and downloads of stories, songs and poems. These are used to develop children's grasp of a wide range of maths related concepts and abilities – which include number facts and values, the four operators, place values, number conservation and the language of maths.
- **Dynamo Maths** is a multisensory programme for 4–11-year-olds that employs three pathways to learning (lesson plans, online activities and worksheets), with each structured in small cumulative steps aimed at gradually building number knowledge. A study conducted by Ann Dowker (2016) looked at the effectiveness of Dynamo Maths for 50 students aged 6–15 years. After 12 weeks of teaching, there was an 11.7 per cent improvement in the students' post-test scores when compared to how they presented prior to the intervention.

Dr Steve Chinn is a leading authority on teaching maths to students with specific learning difficulties. He has written excellent books that guide both specialist and class teachers in hands-on approaches to teaching and reinforcing maths principles and procedures for children who find maths both challenging and daunting. His best-known general book is *The Trouble with Maths* (Chinn, 2016), with other useful books targeting more specific arithmetic domains like learning multiplication tables (Chinn, 2009). Getting to grips with tables is a real headache for many children with literacy and arithmetic difficulties, many of whom have auditory working memory difficulties that mean they cannot easily retain number facts like tables.

As a classroom teacher, you will want to work with the SENCo in devising a suitable teaching programme for the pupil with a specific maths difficulty (whether conducted in the classroom

---

2   See www.addacus.co.uk.

or through withdrawal lessons, and whether individually or in a group). Additionally, teachers can give tips to support staff (including teaching assistants) and parents in reinforcing and practising maths skills, as described in Box 10.1.

Box 10.1: Top tips for learning and practising maths
Basic skills to master and practise in the classroom (and even at home)

- **Counting:** Practise counting out loud from Reception onwards; counting in 1s first, then moving on to counting in 2s, 5s and 10s.
- **Number bonds:** Explain to support staff and parents that these are pairs of numbers that add up to a given number. Children should start by learning and practising the number bonds to 10 (e.g. 2 + 8, 5 + 5 etc.), then up to 20 and so on. Emphasize that for children to work quickly in maths, they have to know their number bonds without thinking about them – they have to be automatic.
- **Multiplication tables:** It does help to learn tables by rote; try singing or chanting them to make them more fun. If you are using the multiplication grid system in the classroom, encourage support staff and parents to follow this also. If the child is really struggling, see Steve Chinn's excellent book *What To Do When You Can't Learn The Times Tables* (Chinn, 2009) for lots of ideas.
- **Memorizing number facts:** There is a lot of evidence that 'talking out loud' through maths steps and operations can be really helpful (as the child gets better at this, they can do it 'under their breath').
- **Fractions:** Children who struggle to grasp the concept of fractions need lots of practical demonstration and explanation. For instance, try cutting up cakes or pieces of fruit into halves, quarters and so on, and talking about how a cake

---

197

cut into two makes two halves and then into four makes four quarters – later on, this practical demonstration can be related to how the fractions are written.

Tips to suggest to parents for practising and reinforcing maths at home:

- Practise every day the new concept or skill the child is learning in class, for say two weeks – and then revisit it every so often to make sure it has been thoroughly learned and, most importantly, remembered.
- Keep practice sessions short – five to ten minutes, depending on the age of the child.
- Do Kumon Maths – explain that this is a systematic, graded and structured maths programme which covers a wide range of ages and abilities. Kumon is not great in itself for teaching concepts in maths, but because it emphasizes a lot of routine worksheet practice, it does ensure that basic skills and operations are thoroughly learned and, most importantly, consolidated and automatized. (This can all be a bit tedious so parents need to be prepared to have 'breaks away' from Kumon and they may need to use an incentive or reward programme to keep the child's motivation going.)
- Use computer-based maths games like *Numbershark*, which teach and reinforce number skills and concepts while presenting to the child as a 'fun' computer game.
- Make maths practical:
  - Suggest to parents that they give their child pocket money so they understand what money is in coin and note form, and teach them to recognize the different coin and note values.
  - In the shop when buying a treat, encourage the child to pay for it themselves using their own

money and then ask them to work out what the change should be.

- In the supermarket, tell the child what a single food item costs and ask them to work out how much they would pay for, say, three of that item.
- Introduce the child to using a calculator while doing the family shop so they can work out what the total bill will be.
- Practise taking measurements when cooking (using jugs, measuring spoons, scales etc.) or buying a new curtain or rug (using a tape measure).
- Teach the child about telling the time and how to use a calendar that relates to their everyday activities (e.g. after-school clubs, parties, outings, sleepovers).

LET'S RECAP

- Children with arithmetic as well as literacy difficulties need systematic interventions aimed at building their cumulative number knowledge and skills from the concrete through to the abstract.
- Class teachers (and teaching assistants, and even some parents) are in a strong position to practise and reinforce basic number skills.
- Worksheet practice and frequent re-visiting of maths concepts and arithmetic procedures ensure that they are retained and consolidated.

CASE STUDY 2: JYOTI, WHO HAS DYSLEXIA AND DYSCALCULIA – TEACHING AND MANAGEMENT

Let us now revisit the case of Joyti, a verbally able nine-year-old girl who has both dyslexia and co-occurring dyscalculia. Her assessment showed that her literacy difficulties (mainly in respect of spelling) are due to her poor phonological processing and her auditory working memory weaknesses. She also has visual spatial difficulties that make it hard for her to grasp visual concepts in maths like geometry, together with auditory working memory difficulties that make mental maths and the retention of number facts challenging for her.

Jyoti's intervention plan

Jyoti has dyslexia that is mainly expressed as spelling difficulties. She has had good phonic decoding instruction which has enabled her to overcome her reading problems, but it may be that her continuing underlying phonological difficulties are behind her obvious spelling problems. She will need continuing literacy support aimed at improving her spelling, both at the word level and as she has to do more free writing. Jyoti also needs specific maths teaching that takes account of her difficulties with number sense and her visual spatial and working memory difficulties. Accommodations in the classroom and for exams are also needed.

Specific recommendations

- A structured phonological awareness training programme that includes auditory-based activities and also 'linkage' exercises that help Jyoti map sounds onto letters (e.g. Sound Linkage).
- A systematic programme that includes learning about spelling-to-sound mappings and rules of English spelling, developing a strong key word spelling vocabulary and introducing Jyoti to more complex spelling units like morphemes.
- Working towards improving Jyoti's spelling in broader

200

writing contexts (i.e. through proofreading and using the computer spellcheck), alongside allowing her to submit some of her course work in word-processed form.

- A maths intervention programme that provides the opportunity for revisiting, reinforcing and practising (using regular worksheets) standard number operations that Jyoti is finding hard to retain and recall. She will also need to address visual concepts within maths, including working with fractions, understanding charts, diagrams, calendars and graphs (and, later on, other visual concepts such as geometry and symmetry and understanding areas, perimeters and volumes and so on).
- Recognition of the impact that Jyoti's short-term auditory/verbal working memory difficulty has on her classroom learning; she is a little girl who will need quite a lot of repetition and reinforcement of new concepts and facts, together with 'chunking' of presented information, and the provision of memory aids to support learning and retention.
- Extra time and use of a laptop computer in formal written examinations should be permitted.
- Jyoti's difficulties and needs should be re-assessed before she starts her GCSE programme.

Future progress and outcome

While Jyoti is likely to experience continuing difficulties in maths and spelling into her senior school years (which will require further intervention), we would nonetheless expect a good overall educational outcome for her in the medium to long term. Positive moderators (or factors) that would be expected to contribute to a good outcome include her high verbal IQ (which helps her compensate for her difficulties), her already good response to early reading intervention, her high levels of motivation and engagement, and, finally, exemplary teacher and parent support.

Treating and supporting children with co-occurring attention difficulties

There are a number of approaches to the treatment of attention deficit with hyperactivity disorder (ADHD) and its often-associated behavioural problems. While prescription medication and psychological interventions are the most commonly used, there has been a recent increasing interest in the use of dietary approaches.

Prescription medication and ADHD

Medications (such as Methylphenidate/Ritalin and Concerta) are recommended for children who have severe attention problems which are most usually accompanied by significant hyperactivity, impulsivity and behaviour problems (especially oppositional-defiant disorder). There have been a lot of research studies in the US that show that prescription medication is highly effective for children with ADHD: not only does it improve children's concentration, it also reduces both their activity level and their behaviour problems. Because ADHD medication has what is called a **short half-life** (i.e. it enters the body's system quickly and is also dispersed and eliminated rapidly), parents often use it strategically or on an as-needs basis (e.g. on school days, during study periods, but not necessarily at weekends or during holidays).

ADHD medication has a reputation of producing serious side-effects, although research has shown that these are rare. However, minor side-effects such as lessening of appetite and sleep problems are quite common. Many families are reluctant to take up the offer of medication because of concerns about side-effects. However, it is important to point out that for many children with very severe ADHD, especially those who have behaviour problems, it is often the best available option – and can be life-changing for children and their families (and teachers too, who have to cope with the high levels of activity and accompanying behavioural difficulties that can in turn seriously disrupt classroom functioning). Having said that, we need also to offer alternative psychological and even dietary treatments, which are often more acceptable to many families – and which appear to work well for children who have milder attention problems and whose behaviour is less affected.

Teacher/parent training and behaviour modification

These psychological interventions for ADHD might include training teachers and parents in effective behavioural-based strategies through:

- **providing information to teachers and parents** about the nature and impact of attention deficits, which helps them better understand and more sympathetically manage the child's difficulties
- **behaviour modification approaches** that can be used at school and at home, such as:
  - using rewards for 'on-task' behaviour, completing tasks they've been asked to do and 'doing what they're told'
  - setting clear boundaries and expectations
  - reducing teacher/parent-child conflict by avoiding confrontation and 'putting space between'
  - modelling (or demonstrating) socially appropriate behaviour
  - restructuring the child's environment as a means of improving attention and behaviour (e.g. by providing quiet work spaces)
  - reducing family hostility levels to provide a quieter and calmer home environment (e.g. advising parents to avoid noisy rows).

  While behavioural approaches don't necessarily lead to the dramatic improvements seen in children who are on prescription medication, they do nonetheless make an impact, not just on the child but also more broadly on classroom and family functioning. See Box 10.2 for behavioural approaches for managing ADHD at school and Box 10.3 for behavioural approaches teachers can advise parents to use at home to manage their child's ADHD
- **coaching interventions** for older children with ADHD. These concentrate largely on improving executive skills such as organization, task initiation and time management. A UK programme, Connections in Mind (www.connectionsinmind.co.uk), provides face-to-face and remote video training, mentoring and support to help

children improve their executive skills that can in turn
lead to improvements in their academic performance.

Box 10.2: Behavioural approaches to
helping concentration in the classroom

The strategies described here can be used in the classroom
to support the child's concentration (and improve their
behaviour too!).

- Give clear boundaries and rules – by for instance
  listing them in bullet point format at the beginning
  of the child's homework diary (ideally, rules need to
  be class general: 'In our class we do...' as opposed
  to, 'You must...').
- Get the child to sit close to the front of the class
  and near the teacher (or a member of the support
  staff).
- Use a child-specific prompt that is non-intrusive,
  like a simple gesture (pointing) or one word to get
  the child's attention or bring them back to the task
  in hand.
- Provide the child with a soft 'squeezy' ball for
  fiddling with – to avoid noisy fiddling activities
  from annoying teachers, support staff and other
  pupils (like tapping on the desk).
- Praise the child when they are 'on task', listening or
  have completed an activity.
- Look at whether it's practical to deal with minor
  infringements by ignoring them.
- For more severe behaviour infringements, ignoring
  might not be enough; try using a short reprimand
  combined with 'time out' (time out involves brief
  removal from whatever the child is doing to a
  boring place such as a corner of the room).
- Provide the child with a one- or two-minute
  warning to help them adjust to changes in routine
  or to switch from one activity to another (i.e.
  alerting the child that one activity is about to end

---

and the other to begin in one or two minutes so that they have time to shift their attention and make the transition).

- Incorporate occasional breaks during an activity – this might be an actual rest break or it could be asking the child to take a message to someone or to clear away some books, or to hand out the pencils.
- Ask a teaching assistant or 'buddy' to be on hand to help the child engage in and complete group- and class-based activities.
- Arrange with the child's parent to set up a home-school diary with stated homework and/or study activities – if the child has worked well on a given activity at school or has been kind and helpful, this can be commented on so that parents can praise the child at home as a further back-up and reinforcement.

Box 10.3: Behavioural approaches to helping concentration at home

Here are some tips you might suggest to the child's parent that they can adopt at home to support their child's attention and to improve behaviour:

- Build routines around the school day (e.g. routines for getting ready in the morning, homework and bedtime). These will help their child know what to expect and they create a structure and organization that helps both attention and learning.
- Make sure their child has access to timetables and schedules that help them know about work requirements – in the form of a school diary or a wall chart in their bedroom.
- Set up a distraction-free space at home for their child to work.
- Set up a home-school diary so that the child and parent both know what is required.

- Set simple goals and even write them down on flashcards or on a whiteboard in the child's room.
- Break up homework and study sessions into smaller 'chunks', each followed by a 'mini-reward'; breaking up tasks into smaller, more manageable steps helps the child to not feel overwhelmed.
- Build in rest breaks that need be only a few minutes in length but can make a big difference to the child's attention.
- Build up listening attention by making sure their child is looking at them, and then by asking them to repeat the instructions back to ensure that the child knows what they're supposed to do.
- Slow the rate of presentation of new materials to be learned and make the instructions shorter too.
- Use 'multi-modal presentation of information' – this means, for instance, accompanying verbal instruction with visual cues, together with giving a clear demonstration of what to do, and guiding the child through it if needed.
- Get their child to verbalize what they are going to do for a particular activity or task – older children might even make bullet-point lists and then tick off each item as it is completed.
- Use a timer or stopwatch when their child works on their homework and during study sessions, so they develop better time awareness and begin to build up their time management skills.
- Vary and rotate tasks and activities (e.g. 15 minutes on maths, then 15 minutes on English and repeat), rather than spending an extended period on one topic or subject.
- Use a low-level sign (a gesture or an agreed prompt word) that is specific and personal to their child and that will prompt them to get back 'on task'.
- Use rewards (e.g. praise, stars or stickers, tokens or treats) for being 'on task' and for task completion.
- Rotate and vary rewards as children with attention problems get satiated and bored quite quickly.

- Make sure that rewards (including praise and feedback) are given frequently and quickly as we know that this increases their effectiveness.

Dietary approaches to ADHD

Many parents of children with concentration difficulties, hyper-activity and difficult behaviours believe their problems are due to eating 'junk food' or foods with 'additives' or 'too much sugar'. I have in the past been very sceptical about the dietary approach to treating ADHD; however, the findings from recent research studies have prompted me to reconsider my stance. These studies have shown that diet modifications and nutritional supplements have a role to play in the management of children with mild-to-moderate attention deficits. There are dietary approaches to the management of ADHD that have been shown to be helpful and that parents can try at home:

- **Restricted elimination diets** involve either removing from the child's diet specific foods to which they appear to be allergic or hypersensitive, or more generally removing foods containing high levels of artificial flavourings and colourings that appear to trigger hyperactivity. Maintaining a healthy diet with few processed foods can result in small, but nonetheless noticeable, improvements in the child's attention and behaviour.
- **Omega 3 (fish oil) supplements** when used long-term – over about six months – have been shown to make children with ADHD less oppositional and aggressive, and to improve their general mood. The main problem for parents in getting their child to take Omega 3 supplements on a regular (daily) basis is that they can have a 'repeating' effect which results in an unpleasant taste. Some manufacturers of Omega 3 supplements are now producing flavoured capsules that are more palatable, which helps the child 'stick with them'.
- **Micronutrients** are vitamins, minerals and amino acids thought to be necessary for optimal brain functioning.

207

One recent scientific study showed that when micronutrients were given to children with ADHD, they showed improved attention, fewer behavioural problems, less aggression and were calmer, more able to be reasoned with and generally happier (Rucklidge *et al.*, 2018). Note that micronutrients of the type used in this study are not available over the counter in the UK, although they may be obtained through the US-based Hardy Nutritionals website. The producers of micronutrients advise parents to seek approval from their GP before use.

LET'S RECAP

- Prescription medications are the treatment of choice for children who have severe ADHD, especially when their attention problems are accompanied by very high levels of overactivity and significant behavioural problems.
- For children with mild to moderate ADHD whose overactivity is not overly excessive and where behaviour problems are comparatively minor, a combination of psychological/behavioural interventions and dietary approaches may be enough to address their difficulties.

CASE STUDY 3: BILLY, WHO HAS DYSLEXIA AND ATTENTION DEFICIT HYPERACTIVITY DISORDER (ADHD) – TEACHING AND MANAGEMENT

Let us now look at the teaching/management programme for Billy, a bright seven-year-old with mild dyslexia (mainly affecting his spelling) and co-occurring attention problems that affect his ability to stay on task, sustain his focus long term and process information quickly and efficiently.

Billy's intervention plan

Billy's mild dyslexia is showing signs of resolving, at least in relation to his reading, which is responding well to special teaching. He also appears to be developing effective compensatory strategies through drawing on his good language skills to help him accurately read words in text and to support his reading comprehension. He will, however, need targeted teaching to address his spelling and associated writing problems. Given that Billy is only seven, it is possible that his attention problems will improve with increasing age and maturity, but it could be helpful to set in place appropriate behavioural supports at home and school and to look at whether a dietary intervention might be helpful. Billy's attention problems and slow processing speed indicate that he might need extra time to complete activities, alongside rest breaks when he is expected to work for long periods.

Specific recommendations

- A systematic spelling programme that incorporates phonics, learning about spelling-to-sound consistencies and acquiring a secure key word spelling vocabulary.
- Home based support that provides opportunities for regular reading out loud (mainly to build reading speed and fluency), reinforcing key word spellings and specific sound–letter units being worked on at school, and using fun-based literacy-oriented computer games, such as *Wordshark*.
- Giving Billy access to technology from age eight onwards so that he can take advantage of the spellcheck and editing facilities that word processing offers.
- Exploring whether a dietary approach could improve Billy's attention – a combination of an additive free diet, and the regular taking of Omega 3 capsules and possibly also micronutrients.
- Providing strategies for Billy's parents and teachers to use to help develop his attention span and reduce

his distractibility – these might include breaking tasks into smaller chunks, providing rest breaks, using rewards (e.g. sticker charts) for staying 'on task' and completing activities, creating a quiet work corner, using timers and feedback charts to help him become more time aware, alerting him to changes in task or routines with a one-minute warning, and using a soft squeezy ball for quiet fiddling.

- Providing Billy with rest breaks and extra time in written tests to accommodate for his attention problems and his slow rate of processing.

Future progress and outcome

While Billy is likely to experience continuing difficulties in spelling and writing skills, it is hoped that these can be managed through 'booster' spelling programmes and use of technology. We would expect an overall good educational outcome for Billy, bearing in mind the positive moderators/factors of high IQ and good verbal skills (which together provide a compensatory resource), his already good response to early reading intervention, his strengths in maths, and high levels of teacher and parental support. However, it will be important to monitor Billy's attention development. If his concentration does not significantly improve as he gets older, and in response to behavioural and dietary interventions, it may be appropriate to refer him to a paediatrician or psychiatrist for consideration of prescription medication.

Treating and supporting children with development coordination disorder/dyspraxia

If a child has severe motor problems, they may be referred for physiotherapy or occupational therapy. The therapist will typically carry out an assessment that looks at the child's gross motor skills (whole body movements), fine motor skills (finger and pencil control), visual perception (being able to discriminate fine visual details), motor planning and organization skills (body movements in an integrated sequence) and sensory integration (the ability to put together information from different senses – such as coordinating hand movements with vision). Generally speaking, if a child is taken on for therapy, the physiotherapist or occupational therapist will adopt either or both of the following two treatment techniques:

- **Sensory integration therapy**, which provides bodily stimulation to improve the sensory and sensory integration deficits thought to underlie the child's motor problems. Suggested activities that are supposed to 'enrich' the sensory systems and promote their integration include swinging, rolling and jumping, joint manipulation, brushing the body and playing with textured toys. However, do bear in mind that there is little scientific evidence that sensory integration leads directly to improvement in classroom skills that depend on motor ability (like handwriting).
- **Teaching the child motor skills** by breaking them down into smaller tasks, guiding them through the steps taken to master each task and giving them plenty of practice and reinforcement until they become skilled at it (e.g. learning how to use a knife and fork correctly).

Many children with mild motor disorders do not have access to sensory or motor programmes such as the ones described above. Rather, it is left to teachers to address the **educational consequences** of the child's motor problems, most usually their difficulties with handwriting and written presentation and organization. If several of your pupils are really struggling with handwriting, maybe consider setting up a special group that is given additional systematic handwriting instruction (delivered by you or a teaching assistant/support worker). Some younger children will need pre-writing activities (such as drawing shapes – see Box 10.4), some may need to work on developing a good posture for handwriting and there will be children whose awkward pencil grip needs to be corrected (see Figure 10.1). Many children will need additional help and practice in letter formation. There is the view that children with handwriting difficulties appear to benefit from an early transition from a printing to a cursive (joined-up) script which can help them overcome problems of uneven letter sizing and spacing. As with most motor skills, the child will need frequent practice to develop improved neatness and speed.

Older children with motor difficulties need support to develop improved written presentation and organization when these skills become increasingly important at secondary school as the child has to produce longer scripts. Children with motor disorders find it really hard to write to speed, which of course they need to do in written exams; providing extra time to complete written assignments and, in particular, tests and examinations will be an important accommodation that needs to be set in place for them. Finally, most schools allow children who have persisting handwriting problems to use alternative means of expressing themselves in written form – through submitting their written assignments in word-processed form, taking a laptop into the classroom for note-taking, and even sitting selected formal exams on a laptop.

See Box 10.4 for tips on how a pupil's motor and writing skills can be supported.

Box 10.4: Tips for helping with motor skills and writing at school (and at home too)

- Make sure the child when writing is sitting upright on a chair with a back support, and at a proper height table or desk.
- Check that the child is using the right pencil grip. The pencil should be held just above the tip, between the thumb and the index finger with the middle finger supporting from beneath; this is called a 'tripod grip' (see Figure 10.1). Children can be helped to hold the pencil the right way by using a pencil with a triangular-shaped barrel/shaft or a slide-on rubber pencil gripper (these need to be used consistently for the child to become practised in using the correct grip).
- Provide pre-writing activities for younger children

---

to improve their fine motor control. These might include drawing geometric shapes, colouring in, drawing their way through a maze, doing pencil-and-paper dot-to-dot games, copy drawing sequences of letter-like shapes, and tracing.

- Use workbooks for copying and practising letter formation.
- Facilitate the practice needed to achieve neat and precise handwriting – sending home handwriting practice sheets or workbooks enables parents to get involved.
- Provide practice in copying passages from a book (at school but at home too) so that the child can just concentrate on the mechanics of writing and presentation and not have to think about anything else. Later on, ask the child to practise writing while an adult dictates a passage so they have to think about spelling and punctuation too.
- Encourage 'beat the clock' exercises to build up speed. Ask the child to copy (and later on write from dictation) four or five sentences as fast as they can; record their time with a clock or stopwatch and enter it on a graph or chart so that you both can see how their speed builds with practice (this is another activity that can be done at home).

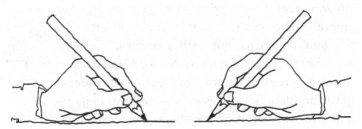

Figure 10.1: How to hold a pen correctly (the tripod grip)

Children who never seem to get the hang of handwriting either legibly or quickly need to increasingly rely on technology, especially as they move towards the end of primary school and on into their secondary school years. If a child is going to be highly laptop dependent, it is crucial that they develop proper touch-typing and keyboarding skills as early as possible – while at primary school and before they get stuck into the one-, two- or three-finger 'hunt and peck' habit. Touch typing is routinely taught in most schools, although some children with motor difficulties will need additional support and practice, for instance, through after-school touch-typing/keyboarding lessons – and backed up by practice at home. *Touch-type Read and Spell* and *Nessy Fingers* are popular software programs that help the child develop touch-typing and word-processing skills.

LET'S RECAP

- Young children with DCD who have handwriting difficulties may need guidance on improving their writing posture and their pencil grip, as well as systematic handwriting instruction.
- Older children will more likely rely on technology to enable them to produce legible written output efficiently and quickly.

CASE STUDY 4: FREDDIE, WHO HAS DYSLEXIA AND DCD/DYSPRAXIA – TEACHING AND MANAGEMENT

You will recall that Freddie is a 12-year-old boy, generally able, with strengths in his verbal abilities and his maths, but with a specific learning difficulty that consists of dyslexia and co-occurring non-verbal difficulties (including significant motor problems). His dyslexia is evident as gaps in his word recognition vocabulary, slow reading speed, very weak spelling and poor phonic decoding. His phonological processing and short-term verbal working memory are also weak. Freddie has visual perceptual, spatial and motor

214

problems that significantly impair his handwriting, speed of writing and general written presentation/organization. Freddie has shown signs of becoming disengaged in the classroom context and there have been frustration-based behaviour problems evident at home.

Freddie's intervention plan

Although Freddie's good functional reading skills (his reading comprehension and silent reading speed) show evidence of compensation, there are gaps in his word recognition, he reads out loud inordinately slowly and he is a reluctant reader. Alongside the need to address these remaining reading problems, Freddie requires interventions that target his poor spelling and written narrative skills. Whether improving his handwriting is a realistic goal at his age is questionable, given that his incorrect pencil grip and poor letter formation may be difficult to modify. It may be more realistic to focus on Freddie taking advantage of technological aids through making the transition to laptop-executed written output, both at home and at school. Accommodations in written examinations will be needed. Finally, Freddie's behavioural difficulties should also be addressed.

Specific recommendations

- Encouraging him to read as much and as broadly as possible in order to increase both his reading vocabulary and his reading speed.
- Providing curriculum-based texts in audio format, so as to capitalize on his keenness for listening to stories.
- Implementing a **repeated reading intervention strategy** to increase his reading speed and fluency.
- Using a structured literacy intervention programme that targets spelling and the development of improved written narrative skills; as well as adopting a phonics-based approach to spelling, Freddie needs to learn about larger spelling units such as morphemes.
- Encouraging Freddie to develop touch-typing, keyboarding and word-processing skills so that he can submit most of his coursework and projects in

laptop-executed format; with touch-typing practice and experience, he may well achieve faster speeds of typing than writing and he will also be able to take advantage of the edit and spellcheck facilities.

- Permitting extra time in formal examinations (in order to accommodate for his slow processing speeds), and providing a scribe or a laptop as appropriate.
- Applying classroom-based accommodations, such as having text-based materials photocopied for him and dropping one of his two foreign languages.
- Setting in place incentive programmes at school to address his disengagement, together with assigning a mentor to play a generally supportive role and more specifically to ensure that he completes and hands in work projects and homework on time.
- Referral to a clinical psychologist for anger management and cognitive behaviour therapy for Freddie, and for advice to his parents on behavioural management.

Future progress and outcome

With the implementation of literacy interventions and class-based accommodations, Freddie should have a positive response and demonstrate improvements in his written language skills. He is likely to have long-standing handwritten output challenges, but with the provision of exam accommodations and increased access to technology, these might be significantly reduced. On a positive note, Freddie shows good capacity to compensate for his dyslexia. Negative moderators/factors include Freddie's disengagement and his frustration-based anger outbursts, though it is hoped that these might be helped through a combination of school-based mentoring and incentive programmes, together with psychological therapies.

KEY MESSAGES TO TAKE AWAY

✓ Children with arithmetic difficulties need systematic teaching programmes that build their number knowledge from the concrete to the abstract – together with plenty of worksheet practice to help them consolidate and automatize arithmetic operations.

✓ Children with mild-to-moderate attention deficit disorders often show improvements in concentration through dietary modifications and nutritional supplements, structuring of their learning environment, the use of behaviour modification programmes and executive coaching (although children with severe ADHD and accompanying behaviour problems will likely need prescription medication).

✓ Children with motor coordination difficulties need systematic handwriting instruction in their early years, but in the long term will improve their written output mainly through access to technology (e.g. laptops).

Chapter 11

Some Broader Management Issues and What to Do If Your Pupil Has a Complex Difficulty

In this chapter I describe how:

→ teachers can encourage parents to be both advocates and active participants in supporting their child's learning difficulties
→ technology, together with classroom, curricula and exam accommodations, can be set in place to ensure that the child with a literacy difficulty is not unfairly disadvantaged
→ children with complex problems might undergo a statutory assessment that results in an Education, Health and Care Plan so that extra resources are made available to them
→ teachers and parents can participate together in the Education, Health and Care Plan process; however, parents may appeal a decision if they feel that their voice is not being heard or that their child's difficulties are not sufficiently recognized and supported.

Broader management issues

Empowering parents

I am a great believer in empowering parents and encouraging them to play an active role in supporting and reinforcing their child's learning – very much in partnership with their child's teachers.

A parent's role in supporting their child with a learning difficulty cannot be overstated; they know their child better than anybody else and they are a permanent fixture throughout their childhood. The knowledgeable and supportive parent can create a positive home-based learning environment for their child, which will massively improve their long-term educational outcome, along with their motivation, self-esteem and confidence. They can also be a great teaching and support resource for teachers to draw on. I've given lots of examples in this and other chapters of how you as a class teacher can bring parents on board to work with their child at home, thus backing-up and reinforcing what you are teaching them in the classroom.

Of course, some parents are better equipped than others to become involved with the management of their child's learning difficulties and to actively support them at home. Some might even be up to delivering prescriptive teaching programmes at home (such as *My Special Alphabet Book* or a parent-friendly phonics programme like Toe by Toe), as well as providing lots of opportunity for their child to practise basic skills within a positive and supportive environment. Other parents are not so able to be proactive at working at home with their child, but even the least confident can be sufficiently supported by teachers in making sure homework is done and reading practised on a reasonably regular basis. It's a question really of getting the best out of what each parent can offer their child in the way of support and encouragement.

Use of technology

In Chapters 9 and 10, I touched on the role played by technology in improving the written output of children who have reading, writing and spelling difficulties. And you will have noted that the intervention plans of Alex, Jyoti, Billy and Freddie contain specific recommendations around the use of laptops. Let's just pull this together more generally.

While the priority in early years education is of course to develop the child's basic reading, handwriting and spelling skills, there is an increasing role for computers, laptops and tablets as children progress through their middle and later school years. We have seen that difficulties with literacy (especially spelling) and motor organization can be life-long challenges. Computers are needed to provide the student with an alternative means of accessing print and producing accurate and legible written output. Children with unusually severe and persisting reading problems may need access to, and training in, voice-activated programmes. Even children with relatively mild spelling and writing problems benefit from submitting course work, projects and essays in word-processed form. Not only does this overcome the problem of difficult-to-read handwriting, it also improves the child's technical accuracy through the use of the editor and spellcheck facilities. Children should be introduced to touch typing at primary school as a foundation skill which enables them, with practice, to achieve fast and accurate written output. Instruction in word processing and encouragement to use the spellcheck are essential to ensure that children make the most of technology. Senior school-age children who have become increasingly speedy and confident on a keyboard may be permitted to take a laptop into the classroom to carry out ongoing course work and note-taking in relevant subjects like English and history. It is usual for students for whom the laptop has become their 'normal way of working' to be allowed to use it in selected written examinations.

Of course, some parents and teachers worry that allowing a child to use technology (including the internet) on a frequent and regular basis might have negative as well as positive consequences. While the use of screens and new technologies is important for children to make social connections and for them to access educational opportunities, there are understandable worries about screen addiction and sexual and other inappropriate content. A recent study has shown that for most children, using screens leads to no significant harm (Dubicka, Martin and Frith, 2019). Indeed, most engage healthily in, and therefore benefit from, internet usage. But there are some children who engage in and experience negative screen and online interactions. These are usually vulnerable youngsters, including those with learning difficulties. If you suspect that a pupil is vulnerable to the negative effects of technology, you could recommend to their parent/s that they should monitor and supervise their child's screen usage, limiting their time spent on activities that are not educationally related while also providing a good model themselves of appropriate usage (e.g. not using mobile phones while eating meals as a family).

Classroom, curricula and exam accommodations

While special teaching programmes are essential to improving specific educational skills, there is an important part to be played by providing **accommodations** to the child with a learning difficulty. This will create for them an 'even playing field' that means they are not unfairly disadvantaged relative to their classmates. The specific accommodations to be set in place will, of course, be dictated by the child's presenting difficulties and their own individual needs. These should be explicitly stated in the child's Individual Learning Plan/Programme, alongside the description of the teaching schemes that are being used. You will have noted that I included classroom and exam accommodations in the intervention plans of our case study children in Chapters 9 and 10.

Classroom-based accommodations might include:

- sitting the child towards the front of the class
- providing quiet study spaces
- assigning a teaching assistant or competent peer mentor (to check on missed instructions or homework requirements)
- providing photocopied notes instead of requiring the child to copy from the black/whiteboard
- setting up a school-to-home-to-school diary to create a conversation between parents and teachers (so ensuring that key skills are practised and reinforced at home and homework completed)
- providing timetables and homework charts that help with time management and planning
- using visual aids like spider diagrams and bullet point check lists that provide **scaffolds** (structures or 'prompts') to improve essay and project technique.

Curricula-based accommodations could include:

- exemption from studying a foreign language (particularly for children who have unusually severe language and literacy difficulties)
- reducing the number of subjects taken at, for instance, GCSE (this being especially relevant for children who have severe difficulties that are likely to include slow processing speed)
- offering a differentiated/modified (usually simplified) curriculum in subjects where the child is unlikely to be able to function at other than a very basic foundation level.

Many children with learning difficulties are able to have access to **accommodations in written examinations.** Two principles are of importance here. The first is that in order to be eligible for such accommodations, it is essential that there is clear 'evidence of need'. This then determines what specific accommodations should be made; this requires documenting a 'history of need' and also demonstrating what is called a 'substantial impairment'. The second principle is that a 'reasonable adjustment' should be made for the 'disabled' student so that they are not substantially disadvantaged in comparison to someone who is not disabled. In the UK, the Joint Council for Qualifications (JCQ) publishes annually an Access Arrangements document that outlines procedures and criteria needed for an individual student to apply for accommodations in examinations such as GCSE and A-levels. Assessments for access arrangements are currently carried out internally (i.e. within the school), although external reports may be taken into account when the SENCo prepares the accommodations documentation. These are the available accommodations:

- **Extra time in exams:** This is usually 25 per cent extra time. To obtain this allowance, the student has to have below average scores on standardized tests, usually measures of reading and writing speed and of cognitive processing. Many students will need considerable practice to ensure that they make full and effective use of allocated extra time.
- **Allocation of a reader:** For a student to be permitted a

reader (or computer reader), they need to have significant reading accuracy and/or speed problems, and also to demonstrate that this has become their 'normal way of working'.

- **Use of a laptop:** Formal testing is not required for the student applying for laptop usage in exams, but they must be able to demonstrate that the laptop has become their 'normal way of working' and that this is in accord with the school's laptop usage policy; the spellcheck is usually disengaged in exams, but a request for spellcheck usage may be made if the student has especially poor spelling (demonstrated as a very low score on a single-word spelling test).

- **Provision of a scribe:** A scribe may be permitted if the student has illegible handwriting (usually accompanied by poor spelling) and is not sufficiently confident or competent to use a word processor.

- **Supervised rest breaks:** These may be available for students with, for instance, diagnosed attention deficit disorders.

LET'S RECAP

- It is impossible to underestimate the importance of parents in creating a positive homework environment and in reinforcing core learning skills in children with learning difficulties.
- Technology (laptops, tablets) have an important role to play for children who experience reading and writing challenges, especially after they reach secondary age.
- Accommodations, both classroom-based and in formal exams, are needed so that children with learning difficulties are not unfairly disadvantaged relative to their peers.

What to do if your pupil has complex difficulties

What we are talking about here are children who have several learning difficulties and also quite often either health or psychiatric/psychological problems – creating a complex and complicated picture for which parents and child need exceptional levels of support. Some examples would include the child with:

- multiple specific learning difficulties, for instance dyslexia, dyscalculia, development coordination disorder (DCD) and ADHD (all at the same time)
- wide-ranging learning difficulties that are associated with neurological problems, like having cerebral palsy, epilepsy or a brain tumour
- complex disorders such as autistic spectrum disorder (ASD).

If a pupil has severe and complex difficulties, you (and the SENCo and headteacher) may want to consider applying to the local education authority for a statutory assessment that leads to an Education, Health and Care Plan (EHC Plan); see Box 11.1 for a summary. A fuller description of the EHC process can be found on the website of the Independent Provider of Special Education Advice (IPSEA), which is a registered charity that provides free and independent advice for all kinds of special educational needs and disabilities (www.ipsea.org.uk).

Box 11.1: The Education, Health and Care Plan

The EHC Plan is a legal document which describes a child's or young person's special educational needs, the support they should receive and the outcomes they would like to achieve. The special educational needs described in the EHC Plan must be provided for by the child's local authority (LA). Not only does the EHC Plan provide extra learning support, but it also gives parents more choice about alternative school placements or educational settings. The first step in the process is requesting an EHC needs assessment.

Applying for an EHC needs assessment

The assessment is requested by the child's school (in conjunction with their parents) for a child who is thought to be in need of exceptional special educational provision. This is in the form of a letter to the LA, which must reply within six weeks. The LA may or may not agree to the assessment; if they do not, there is a right to appeal through a tribunal process.

What is involved in the EHC needs assessment?

The LA must seek advice from a range of sources:

1. The child's parent or the young person themselves.
2. Educational reports from the child's teachers.
3. Medical advice and information from a healthcare professional.
4. Psychological advice and information from an educational psychologist.
5. Advice and information in relation to social care.
6. Advice and information from any other person the LA sees as appropriate.

Teachers or parents may request information from a particular specialist, such as a speech and language therapist, an occupational therapist or a psychiatrist, and recently completed reports from other sources may be submitted (which can include private assessment reports). Advice sought should address the child's needs, the specific educational provision required to meet those needs and the outcome this provision aims to achieve. An EHC Plan should be issued within a maximum of 20 weeks from the request for assessment. If the LA decides not to issue an EHC Plan, parents may appeal through the Special Educational Needs and Disability (SEND) Tribunal process.

Appealing against an EHC needs decision

The SEND Tribunal is an independent national tribunal which hears parents' appeals against decisions by LAs in regard to their child's special educational needs. The Tribunal has the power to order the LA to carry out an EHC needs assessment, to issue an EHC Plan and to amend existing EHC Plans. The LA must comply with the orders made by the Tribunal. The SEND Tribunal looks at the evidence put before it and decides whether the LA followed the law and the SEND Code of Practice. It then makes a decision based on what is right for the child at the date of the hearing. The majority of requests for appeal are settled before the Tribunal through mediation with the LA; for instance, the Department for Education reported in 2017 that around 75 per cent of cases are agreed through mediation (Department for Education, 2017). The SEND Tribunal publishes a free booklet, *How to Appeal*, which can be accessed on their website.

If a parent wants to proceed with an appeal without legal representation they may do so, but it is possible to apply for legal aid if they wish to appoint a lawyer to represent them at the hearing. The IPSEA Tribunal Helpline is able to provide advice on how to submit an appeal for parents who have not appointed a lawyer.

Sometimes parents and teachers may disagree as to whether or not an EHC Plan is needed for a particular child. Realistically, unless a child has a severe and complex learning presentation, usually with accompanying health or psychological problems, it is unlikely that the LA will agree to the assessment taking place. Parents may need advice and support from assessors, SENCos and teachers to enable them to come to the right decision as to whether or not to pursue an EHC Plan (or a resultant appeal). The child who presents with dyslexia (and few other learning issues or problems) will be unlikely to be granted an EHC Plan because it is assumed that their needs can be met within existing school-based learning support resources. The EHC process works better and is more likely to be successful if parents and teachers alike agree that it is the right course of action for a given child whose complex needs cannot be met within the school's existing learning support (including financial) resources.

The EHC process has been met with a lot of criticisms. An article by Louise Tickle, published in *The Guardian* newspaper on 5 September 2017, discussed Department for Education figures for that year showing that 4000 children with approved EHC Plans received no additional support. It is unlikely that matters have improved much since. In 2022, just 49.2 per cent of new EHC Plan applications were processed in the mandatory 20-week deadline (Department for Education, 2023). Finally, many parents report that pursuing an appeal causes them stress and often financial hardship (if they appoint a lawyer and request additional private assessments); this is certainly something I have observed, having represented parents as an expert witness at a number of appeal tribunals.

As an example of the level of complexity needed for a child to qualify for an Education, Health and Care Plan, I will describe one final case study, Leila, who was born extremely prematurely and who has, as a consequence, multiple learning and psychological/psychiatric difficulties.

As you read through Leila's case study, bear in mind some **facts about children born at extreme prematurity**:

- Children born extremely prematurely are significantly at risk of experiencing brain damage that results in a wide range of persisting cognitive and educational difficulties.
- Having said that, the outcome for individual children varies a great deal, with one-third of extremely premature children having severe and pervasive learning difficulties, one third having mild-to-moderate (and possibly more selective) difficulties, while the remaining third present with few or even no learning compromises.
- Some premature children who have a localized brain injury show evidence of a compensatory process called **functional reorganization**; this is made possible by the fact that the infant brain is 'plastic' (or flexible) so that if the damage is to the language regions of the brain, other regions can take over that skill so that language is preserved (however, other abilities, in particular non-verbal skills and processing speed, may become

diminished through being **crowded out** in what is now a reduced 'neural space').

LEILA

Leila had been born very prematurely, at 29 weeks, weighing just 750 grams; her prematurity was occurring in the context of intra-uterine growth retardation. She was admitted to the special care baby unit where she suffered a series of seizures; she then continued in this setting on a ventilator for a total of two months. Leila received courses of physiotherapy, occupational therapy and speech and language therapy as a pre-schooler. She was at the time of the first assessment (when aged five) attending a local state school where her teachers expressed concern about her poor oral communication skills, her very slow educational progress and her immature (and at times difficult) behaviour.

Leila underwent four cognitive-educational evaluations over a five-year period, with the final assessment taking place when she was ten years old. During her primary schooling, she exhibited difficulties within the domains of language, visual motor skill, educational attainments, attention and also in respect of behaviour and socialization. When she was seven years old, her school applied to the local authority for a statutory assessment that eventually resulted in an Education, Health and Care Plan, which was completed when she was eight years old. This provided funding for a part-time learning support assistant for 15 hours/week to support Leila during core lessons. Her curriculum was differentiated, most obviously in maths but also to some degree in literacy. Additional funding was provided so that Leila could receive one-to-one targeted intervention in maths and literacy, and also speech and language therapy in 'blocks'.

Intellectual functioning

At Leila's first two assessments (aged 5 and 7 years), she had recorded Verbal Comprehension Indices /Verbal IQ scores in the low-average range (80s). However, at the two later assessments (aged 9 and 10 years), her Verbal Comprehension Index/Verbal

IQ scores had risen to a comfortably average level (around the 100 mark). Her Nonverbal IQ was low at all four assessments, with index scores ranging from 80 to 85. Her Processing Speed Index at the age 10 assessment was a low-average 80.

Educational attainments

When Leila was first assessed aged five years, she was essentially a non-reader and she was able to demonstrate only very basic concrete number skills. When she was re-assessed at age seven, her literacy and numeracy skills were beginning to develop, albeit slowly. Her attainments at the last two assessments are given below:

Educational skill (WIAT-II and YARC)	Age nine standard score	Age ten standard score
Numerical Operations	83	72
Mathematics Reasoning	60	60
Single Word Reading	82	86
Prose Reading Accuracy	82	90
Reading Speed	85	90
Pseudoword Decoding	80	88
Reading Comprehension	87	100
Spelling	80	75

Diagnostic tests given at age ten years

- **Dyslexia-sensitive tests:** Leila scored at a comfortably average level (standard score = 100) on a measure of phonological **awareness** (CTOPP2 Phoneme Elision), having greatly improved since the previous year (standard score = 80). She did, however, score at a below average level (standard score = 75) on a measure of phonological **processing** (CTOPP2 Rapid Letter Naming).
- **Short-term verbal working memory:** Leila has significant short-term verbal working memory

limitations, as evidenced by her standard score of 70 on WISC Digit Span.

- **Dyspraxia-sensitive tests:** Leila scored at a low average level (standard score of 83) on WISC Coding, a measure of speed of graphomotor processing, and at a well below average level (standard score of under 70) on the Rey Complex Figure Copy Test, a measure of motor organization.
- **Dyscalculia-sensitive tests:** Leila was administered three subtests from the Test of Basic Arithmetic and Numeracy Skills (TOBANS), specifically the measures of numerosity (i.e. dot counting, dot comparison and digit comparison) on which she achieved low average to below average standard scores of between 65 and 80.
- **Attention skills:** Leila obtained a below average standard score of 75 on Score!, a measure of sustained attention from the Test of Everyday Attention for Children (TEA-Ch).

Formulation

Leila is a girl of normal intelligence with definite relative strengths within the important academically predictive verbal ability domain. Given the increase in her verbal IQ over the last five years (to a now average level), contrasted with her relatively weaker non-verbal ability and processing speed, she may have undergone brain-based functional reorganization with accompanying cognitive crowding; this has resulted in good preservation of her language skills but at the cost of diminished non-verbal ability and processing speed.

Leila exhibits the underlying cognitive deficits typically seen in children with **dyslexia**, notably selective weaknesses in short-term verbal working memory, phonological processing and phonic decoding. She has nonetheless made steady gains in her single-word reading over the last year or so. Her prose reading accuracy, reading speed and decoding have shown improvements over the course of the last 15 months in response to targeted intervention. Her reading comprehension (being age appropriate) is a relative strength, and is likely to be supported by her good oral language. She has made little if any progress in her spelling.

Leila has additional (co-occurring) specific learning difficulties beyond her dyslexia. She has a mild-to-moderate **attention deficit hyperactivity disorder (ADHD)**, evident on both diagnostic testing and on behavioural observation. She also has **dyspraxia/ developmental coordination disorder (DCD)**; her graphomotor and motor organization skills are poor and these impact on her handwriting speed and quality. Finally, Leila has severe **dyscalculia**; she has very poor numerosity, which explains her inability to progress in maths over the last year or so.

In conclusion, Leila has a complex learning disorder of neurodevelopmental origin which results in a diverse range of cognitive, educational, motor and attentional problems. Although currently presenting as being of normal ability and average verbal intelligence, she has a multi-component specific learning difficulty that comprises several co-occurring disorders, specifically moderate dyslexia, mild-to-moderate dyspraxia, severe dyscalculia and mild-to-moderate ADHD. Leila's parents and teachers report that she exhibits at times severe behaviour difficulties, both at home and at school.

Leila's intervention plan

Leila's senior schooling needs are now under consideration. She will need a revision of her EHC Plan during her last year at primary school in order to determine her current special needs and how these should be met when she proceeds to her next school. It will be important for her to receive a high level of ongoing in-class learning support and accommodations, together with specific interventions for literacy and numeracy, throughout her senior school years.

Specific recommendations for intervention and management

- Leila's EHC Plan should continue throughout her senior schooling, with annual reviews taking place as statutorily required.

- Access to 15 hours/week of learning support assistance during core (academic) lessons should be maintained at senior school; this is important not just to enable her to access her curriculum but also to support her compromised attention and short-term memory skills.
- Leila will need access to an individualized literacy support programme that targets her continuing weak decoding, slow reading speed and especially her marked spelling difficulties.
- Leila will require a differentiated maths curriculum which takes account of her minimal numerical attainments, together with daily one-to-one intervention.
- Leila will need access to technological aids and to be given explicit instruction in their application to enable her to improve the quality of her written output.
- Leila's attention skills to date have been sufficiently supported through in-class provisions; however, given the increased attentional and organization demands of senior school, it may be necessary to consider coaching/mentoring support and perhaps also the use of prescription medication.
- Leila will require classroom accommodations to be set in place to support, and to compensate for, her poor verbal working memory (to include cueing, repetition, 'chunking' of information, reduced complexity and length of instructions, and scaffolding).
- Leila will eventually need full accommodations when she takes formal tests and examinations, which could include having questions read to her, extra time, access to a scribe, and rest breaks as needed.
- Leila and her parents and teachers will need support and advice from a clinical psychologist so that her home- and class-based behaviour can be improved.

Prognosis and outcome

Given the complexity of Leila's cognitive/educational profile, her very slow progress in maths and the observation that extremely premature children tend to have learning difficulties that

233

persist through to the adult years, statements about future progress should be guarded and expectations for medium- and long-term outcome kept appropriately conservative. While Leila taking GCSEs is not out of the question, it will be necessary for her to work towards a reduced number of subjects so as not to overload her compromised verbal working memory, attention and processing speed skills. Core subjects will need to be taken at 'foundation' level, and options selected according to her emerging strengths and interests. Post-GCSE, Leila's EHC Plan should be maintained so that she is able to proceed to a college with high levels of special needs provision.

KEY MESSAGES TO TAKE AWAY

✓ Broader management issues relevant to almost all children with specific learning difficulties include the roles of parents acting as advocates for their child and supporting them at home – alongside teachers promoting the use of technology to improve written output and setting in place appropriate accommodations in the classroom and in written examinations.

✓ Children with complex learning problems (and especially those with accompanying health and psychological problems) require multi-domain assessments and high levels of learning support, specialist interventions and therapeutic input for the duration of their formal schooling – which is most realistically attainable through an Education, Health and Care Plan.

Closing Comments

Now that you have reached the end of this book, I hope that you as a teacher feel that you have, first, the knowledge that enables you to better understand and appreciate the difficulties the pupil with a literacy difficulty experiences (which formed the first half of the book) and, second, the tools that put you in a strong position to support and promote their learning (the second half of the book). Enhancing children's literacy skills not only improves their opportunities in later life but also helps develop and maintain their psychological well-being.

A key message I wanted to get across in this book is the importance of class teachers creating partnerships with assessors, SENCos, specialist teachers, support staff and parents. Working with specialists and SENCos enables you as a member of a team to plan intervention programmes and develop management strategies that improve the child's learning and their literacy outcome. As a busy class teacher with 20–30 children's educational needs to address, it is very difficult to deliver individualized teaching programmes yourself – which is where drawing on resources such as teaching assistants, classroom volunteers and parents is critical. While trained and supervised teaching assistants can often deliver prescriptive teaching programmes successfully, arguably the most important role that support staff (and parents) can play is in providing practice and reinforcement of specific skills, so that these become consolidated and automatized.

The individual child's difficulties (and their strengths too) will look different according to the age and the stage of learning that they're at. So, keep this book on hand as a reference source that you can revisit from time to time, and do dip in and out of the sections that are relevant to your pupil's current issues and needs.

Following on from here, I have made some suggestions for further reading and organizations that provide ongoing support, advice and guidance to those working with children with literacy difficulties (and their co-occurring problems). There is also a glossary of terms used in the book, and a list of references.

Glossary

Alphabetic principle/Phonological linkage: The child's understanding that the letters they see in print stand for the individual sounds they hear in spoken words.

Attention deficit hyperactivity disorder/ADHD: A developmental disorder in which a child has difficulty in focusing and sustaining attention; it is often accompanied by high levels of activity, distractibility and impulsivity.

Correlation: A statistical term that describes the relationship or connection between two or more things; a correlation expressed as a number describes the strength of the connection, so, for example, a correlation of 0.8 indicates a strong connection while a correlation of 0.2 indicates a weak connection.

Developmental coordination disorder/DCD (dyspraxia): A developmental disorder in which a child's difficulties with visual motor skill cause problems with handwriting, written presentation and organization.

Developmental language disorder/DLD: A learning difficulty in which a child's oral language skills are much poorer than their non-verbal abilities (which are usually within the average range); these children may have difficulty in understanding spoken language or expressing themselves verbally (or both).

Domain general deficit: A cognitive deficit seen across a wide range of different developmental/learning disorders; the most commonly described domain general deficit is slow processing speed.

Dyscalculia (specific arithmetic disorder): A learning difficulty in which a child finds it hard to acquire maths concepts and to calculate with numbers accurately and efficiently.

Dyslexia: Describes a word-level reading problem; it is caused by underlying phonological processing difficulties that impair the development of phonic decoding skills needed to learn to read and spell accurately and efficiently.

Full Scale IQ: A composite figure that reflects an individual's overall ability and is expressed as an index score with a mean of 100; it is based on a number of measures that assess different components of learning (usually verbal and non-verbal abilities, working memory and processing speed).

Graphemes: How we represent phonemes as written letters; they can be single letters (b, t, s) or letter combinations (sh, oo, ee).

Individual Educational Plan (IEP): A school document that summarizes a child's learning difficulties and sets out what is needed to support them; it should include targets, learning support strategies, criteria for successful achievement and a record of when criteria are met.

Listening comprehension: Children's understanding of language in spoken form; it can be measured by, for instance, telling a child a story and asking them either to tell it back in as much detail as they can remember or to answer questions about the content of the story.

Longitudinal research: When the same group of individuals is studied over a period of time to look at how they develop and particularly to find out which early measured factors have the strongest predictive relationship with later measured factors – for example, which pre-school learning skills best predict children's later ease of learning to read.

Morphemes: 'Units of meaning'. For example, in the word 'unforgettable', there are three morphemes – un forget and able – which, when combined, give the word its full meaning. Morphemes such as prefixes like re- and un- and word endings like -ment, -ness -ful, which occur in multi-syllabic words, are usually consistently spelled and so can help children become better rule-based spellers.

Naming speed: By asking the child to name letters, numbers, pictures or colours as fast as they can, we can capture the speed and efficiency with which they are able to retrieve or 'get at' phonological representations of words in their memory store.

Numerosity: A child's 'number sense' or their awareness of the magnitude of numbers; numerosity can be measured by, for instance, asking the child which is the bigger of two numbers or to decide which of two boxes contains the most dots (at speed).

Onsets and rimes: The onset of a single-syllable word is the initial consonant/s and the rime is the following vowel and final consonant/s (if any), so in the word 'stop', the onset is 'st' and the rime is 'op'. An understanding of onset and rime is needed for children to learn how to spell by analogy (or word families), for example 'fright', 'sight', 'might', 'light' all share the same rime ('ight') but have different onsets.

Phoneme: The smallest pronounceable unit of sound – sounds like 'ee', 'p', 't', 'o' are examples of phonemes.

Phonic decoding: A child's ability to 'sound out' printed words and then to blend these sounds so that they pronounce the word correctly.

Phonological awareness: A child's understanding of the sound structure of spoken words and their ability to recognize, process and manipulate these sounds; it is a powerful predictor of ease of learning to read.

Phonological memory/Auditory/verbal working memory: A term used to describe how we code or represent speech sounds in our short-term verbal memory store; it can be measured by asking children to, for example, repeat a sequence of random digits forwards or backwards or to repeat a long nonsense word.

Prognosis/Outcome: Predicting the child's likely future rate of progress and how they will look later on in life. Prognoses and outcomes may be positive or negative and depend not just on cognitive factors or moderators but also on environmental factors (like early versus late identification, quality of teaching and level of parental support).

Scaled score: Describes an individual's performance on a test or measure, with a mean or average of 10; a score of 10 indicates average performance, a score of well below 10 indicates poor performance and a score of well above 10 means good performance.

Standard score or index score: Describes an individual's performance on a test or measure. A standard or index score has a mean (or average) of 100; a score of 100 indicates average performance, a score of well above 100 indicates good performance and a score of well below 100 indicates poor performance.

References

Beck, I.L., McKeown, M.G. and Kucan, L. (2002) *Bringing Words to Life: Robust Vocabulary Instruction*. New York, NY: Guilford Press.

Bookstart (2014) *Family reading habits and the impact of Bookstart*. Liberty Venn, The Children's Book Project. London, UK.

Brooks, G. (2016) *What works for children and young people with literacy difficulties? The effectiveness of intervention schemes*, fifth edition. Evesham: Dyslexia- SpLD Trust.

Byrne, B. (1998) *The Foundation of Literacy: The Child's Acquisition of the Alphabetic Principle*. Hove: Psychology Press.

Caravolas, M., Lervag, A., Mousikou, P., Efrin, C. et al. (2012) 'Common patterns of prediction of literacy development in different alphabetic orthographies.' *Psychological Science*, 23(6), 678–686.

Chinn, S. (2009) *What To Do When You Can't Learn The Times Tables*. London: Egon Publishers.

Chinn, S. (2016) *The Trouble With Maths: A Practical Guide to Helping Learners with Numeracy Difficulties*. London: Taylor and Francis.

Clarke, P., Snowling, M., Truelove, E. and Hulme, C. (2010) 'Ameliorating children's reading comprehension difficulties: A randomised controlled trial.' *Psychological Science*, 21(8), 1106–1116.

Clarke, P., Truelove, E., Hulme, C. and Snowling, M. (2014) *Developing Reading Comprehension*. Chichester: Wiley Blackwell.

Cooper, M., Hammerton, G., Collishaw, S., Langley, K. *et al.* (2018) 'Investigating late-onset ADHD: A population cohort investigation.' *Journal of Child Psychology and Psychiatry*, 59(10), 1105–1113.

Cunningham, A. and Stanovich, K. (1997) 'Early reading acquisition and its relation to reading experience and ability 10 years later.' *Developmental Psychology*, 33(6), 934–935.

Department for Education (2017) Statements of SEN and EHC Plans, England 2017. www.gov.uk/government/statistics/statements-of-sen-and-ehc-plans-england-2017.

Department for Education (2023) Education, Health and Care plans. Reporting Year 2023. https://explore-education-statistics.service.gov.uk/find-statistics/education-health-and-care-plans.

Dowker, A. (2016) 'An independent evaluation of the effectiveness of Dynamo Maths.' www.dynamomaths.co.uk/evidence.

Dubicka, B., Martin, J. and Frith, J. (2019) 'Screen time, social media and developing brains: A cause for good or corrupting young minds.' *Child and Adolescent Mental Health*, 24, 203–204.

Elliott, J. and Grigorenko, E. (2014) *The Dyslexia Debate*. New York, NY: Cambridge University Press.

Gathercole, S. and Packiam-Alloway, T. (2008) *Working Memory and Learning: A Practical Guide for Teachers*. London: Sage.

Harris, K.R., Graham, S., Mason, L. and Friedlander, B. (2008) *Powerful Writing Strategies for All Students*. Baltimore, MD: Paul Brookes Publishing.

Hatcher, P., Duff, F. and Hulme, C. (2014) *Sound Linkage*. Chichester: Wiley Blackwell.

Kelly, K. and Phillips, S. (2022) *Teaching Literacy to Learners with Dyslexia: A Multisensory Approach*. London: Corwin (Sage).

Melby-Lervag, M. and Hulme, C. (2013) 'Is working memory training effective? A meta-analytic review.' *Developmental Psychology*, 49(2), 270–291.

Moody, S. (2004) *Dyslexia: A Teenager's Guide*. London: Vermilion Press.

Moseley, D. and Nicol, C. (1995) *ACE Spelling Dictionary*. Cambridge: LDA.

Muter, V. and Snowling, M.J. (1998) 'Concurrent and longitudinal predictors of reading: The role of metalinguistic and short-term memory skills.' *Reading Research Quarterly*, 33(3), 320–337.

Muter, V. and Likierman, H. (2022) *My Special Alphabet Book*. London: Jessica Kingsley Publishers.

Muter, V., Hulme, C., Snowling, M.J. and Taylor, S. (1998) 'Segmentation not rhyming predicts early progress in learning to read.' *Journal of Experimental Child Psychology*, 71(7), 3–27.

Muter, V., Hulme, C., Snowling, M.J. and Stevenson, J. (2004) 'Phonemes, rimes, vocabulary and grammatical skills as foundations of early reading development: Evidence from a longitudinal study.' *Developmental Psychology*, 40(5), 663–681.

Nunes, T. and Bryant, P. (2009) *Children's Reading and Spelling: Beyond the First Steps*. Chichester: Wiley-Blackwell.

Rucklidge, J.J., Eggleston, M.J.F., Johnstone, J.M., Darling, K. *et al.* (2018) 'Vitamin-mineral treatment improves aggression and emotional regulation in children with ADHD: A fully blinded, randomized, placebo-controlled trial.' *Journal of Child Psychology and Psychiatry*, 59(3), 232–246.

Seymour, P.H.K. (2005) 'Early Reading Development in European Orthographies.' In M.J. Snowling and C. Hulme (eds), *The Science of Reading: A Handbook*. Oxford: Blackwell Publishing.

Snowling, M.J. (2000) *Dyslexia*. Oxford: Blackwell.

Snowling, M.J., Gallagher, A. and Frith, U. (2003) 'Family risk of dyslexia is continuous: Individual differences in the precursors of reading skill.' *Child Development*, 74(2), 358–373.

Snowling, M.J., Muter, V. and Carroll, J. (2007) 'Children at family risk of dyslexia: A follow-up in early adolescence.' *Journal of Child Psychology and Psychiatry*, 48(6), 609–618.

Snowling, M.J., Duff, F.J., Nash, H.M. and Hulme, C. (2016) 'Language profiles and literacy outcomes of children with resolving, emerging or persisting language impairments.' *Journal of Child Psychology and Psychiatry*, 57(12), 1360–1369.

Strong, G., Torgesen, C., Torgesen, D. and Hulme, C. (2011) 'A systematic meta-analytic review of evidence of the effectiveness of the Fast ForWord Language Intervention Program.' *Journal of Child Psychology and Psychiatry*, 52(3), 224–235.

Wechsler, D. (2014) *Wechsler Pre-School and Primary Scale of Intelligence*, 4th edition (WPPSI-IV). London: Pearson.

Wechsler, D. (2016) *Wechsler Intelligence Scale for Children*, 5th edition (WISC-V). London: Pearson.

Wechsler, D. (2017) *Wechsler Individual Achievement Test*, 3rd edition (WIAT-III). London: Pearson.

Resources

Books, programmes and workbooks that class teachers (and some parents) can use

Barrington-Stoke Publishers: barringtonstoke.co.uk. Publishes fiction and non-fiction adapted to different reading levels for reluctant, under-confident and dyslexic children and teens.

Beck, I.L., McKeown, M.G. and Kucan, L. (2013) *Bringing Words to Life: Robust Vocabulary Instruction*. New York, NY: Guilford Press (2nd edition). Offers a very practical but systematic approach to improving children's vocabulary knowledge – which is important to academic learning in general and key to having good reading comprehension.

Cowling, H. and Cowling, K. (1993) *Ioe by Toe: A Highly Structured Multisensory Phonetic Based Approach To Literacy*. https://toe-by-toe.co.uk. This is a phonic-based teaching programme that many parents have told me is easily usable at home.

Gathercole, S. and Packiam-Alloway, T. (2008). *Working Memory and Learning: A Practical Guide for Teachers*. London: Sage. Although designed for teachers to use in the classroom, this book has lots of practical suggestions for supporting working memory in the home context too.

Kumon Maths: www.kumon.co.uk. Offers after-school programmes for children of all ages; this worksheet-oriented programme is great for establishing, reinforcing and consolidating basic number operations, but is less good at teaching broader maths concepts.

Listening Books: www.listening-books.org.uk. Offers a wide range of books on audio, covering fiction and factual subjects useful for school learning.

Moody, S. (2004). *Dyslexia: A Teenager's Guide*. London: Vermilion Press. An excellent guide for teenagers and their parents as to how to cope with being dyslexic at secondary school.

Muter, V. and Likierman, H. (2022) *My Special Alphabet Book*. London: Jessica Kingsley Publishers. A workbook aimed at teaching the foundation skills for making a good start in learning to read. It is designed for early years teachers and for parents to use with children at risk of dyslexia or who are slow in acquiring language skills – it covers the basics of learning the alphabet, simple phonological skills and oral language.

Nessy Fingers (www.nessy.com) is a computer program that teaches touch-typing and keyboarding skills to children aged seven years and above. The individual keys are introduced alphabetically in a structured sequence of word lists, with the aim of supporting not just typing but also spelling skills.

Reid, G., McIntosh, M. and Clark, J. (2022) *Practical Activities and Ideas for Parents of Dyslexic Kids and Teens*. London: Jessica Kingsley Publishers. This workbook provides lots of activities and games to help improve literacy skills in children from aged seven years or so through to adolescence.

Snowling, M. (2019) *Dyslexia: A Very Short Introduction*. Oxford: Blackwell. A very good introduction to what dyslexia is, written by the UK's leading authority on dyslexia.

Touch-type Read and Spell (TTRS): https://ttrsonline.com. TTRS is a modular-based computer program that teaches touch typing, reading and spelling skills and is suitable for home- as well as school-based use.

Wordshark and *Numbershark*: www.wordshark.co.uk. These are fun game-styled computer programs to supplement face-to-face learning in literacy and numeracy.

Support and resource organizations

AFASIC/Association for All Speech Impaired Children (www.afasic. org.uk) provides information, support and advice for individuals who have a speech and/or language disorder and their families; AFASIC has a telephone and email helpline, runs workshops and courses and provides links to access speech and language therapy services.

British Dyslexia Association (www.bdadyslexia.org.uk) offers advice and support (through a telephone and email helpline) to individuals with dyslexia and their families, teachers and employers; it also offers specific services such as assessments and accredited courses.

Connections in Mind (www.connectionsinmind.co.uk) provides coaching for independent learning for children and adolescents who have executive and attention problems that impact both academically and behaviourally. It provides a bespoke skill training service to the young person through face-to-face coaching, Skype, email and text, and through parent support.

Dyscalculia Information Centre (www.dyscalculia.me.uk) provides information to parents and teachers about dyscalculia and offers advice on teaching materials (includes an online shop), though this organization does not have the extensive resources of the other associations listed here.

Dyslexia Action (https://dyslexiaactionorg.uk) provides learning resources to teachers and can be contacted by phone, email or social media

Dyspraxia Foundation (https://dyspraxiafoundation.org.uk) supports and advises individuals with dyspraxia/DCD and their families through its locally based events and workshops, as well as offering a telephone and email helpline resource.

National Attention Deficit Disorder Information and Support Service (ADDISS) (www.addiss.co.uk) offers information, support and advice through its telephone and email helpline, bookstore and conferences, and training courses for parents and professionals.

Professional organizations

Association of Speech and Language Therapists in Independent Practice (ASLTIP) (https://beta.helpwithtalking.com) provides information and a contact point for members of the public searching for an independent (i.e. private practising) speech and language therapist.

British Psychological Society (BPS) (www.bps.org.uk) is the professional association for chartered clinical and educational psychologists and also neuropsychologists. There is a directory of chartered psychologists which can help members of the public locate a chartered psychologist offering services in their area (note that the Health and Care Professions Council is the regulator for practising psychologists in the UK).

Chartered Society of Physiotherapists (CSP) (www.csp.org.uk) is the professional body for chartered physiotherapists in the UK. The society provides information to the public about accessing NHS and private practising physiotherapists in their area.

National Online Psychiatry Service (www.psychiatry-uk.com/psychiatry-for-children) is an example of an online service to the public that can arrange private psychiatric consultation in their area.

Professional Association for Teachers of Students with Specific Learning Difficulties (Patoss) (www.patoss-dyslexia.org.uk) specializes in training and supporting teachers of individuals with specific learning difficulties through accredited training and continuing professional development courses. It also provides UK-wide lists of teachers and tutors for individuals and parents to contact.

Royal College of Occupational Therapists (RCOT) (www.rcot.co.uk) is the professional body for occupational therapists in the UK. There is an online directory to enable members of the public to locate an occupational therapist in their area.

Royal College of Psychiatrists (RCP) (ww.rcpsych.ac.uk) is the professional body for child psychiatrists in the UK. Referral to a child psychiatrist at NHS CAMHS (Child and Adolescent Mental Health Services) can be made through the child's and family's GP.

Royal College of Speech and Language Therapists (RCSLT) (www.rcslt.org.uk) is the professional body for speech and language therapists in the UK.

Index

accommodations 222–4
ACE Spelling Dictionary
    (Moseley & Nicol) 179
Addacus 196
ADHD 90–5, 133–4, 135–6,
    139–42, 202–10
alphabetic principle
    28–9, 32–3, 37–8
alternative therapies 163–5
analogies 156–7
artificial intelligence 29–32
assessments for co-occurring
    difficulties
  for ADHD 135–6
  case studies for 137–48
  for dyscalculia 135
  for dyspraxia 136–7
  for second language
      learners 144–7
assessments for literacy
    difficulties
  background information for
      113
  case studies for 124–30
  for developmental language
      disorder 117–18
  for dyslexia 117, 123
  educational skills tests 116
  IQ tests 113–16
  for second language
      learners 119–20
  understanding assessor's
      report 120–2
at-risk children 55, 57,
    72–3, 76, 80, 85
auditory working memory
    38–9, 160–1, 186–7

Beck, Isabel 182
behavioural model of
    dyslexia 58–9
biological model of dyslexia
    54–6, 70–2
Bookstart 45
brain difference in
    dyslexia 55–6, 71
*Bringing Words to Life: Robust
    Vocabulary Instruction*
    (Beck *et al.*) 182
Brooks, G. 173
Bryant, P. 157
Byrne, Brian 28

Caravolas, Marketa 43
case studies
  on ADHD 94–5, 208–10
  on assessments for co-occurring
      difficulties 124–30
  on assessments for literacy
      difficulties 124–30
  on complex difficulties 229–34
  on developmental coordination
      disorder 98–9, 214–16
  on developmental language
      disorder 78–80
  on dyscalculia 89–90, 200–1
  on dyslexia 62–3, 78–80,
      89–90, 94–5, 98–9
  on dyspraxia 98–9, 214–16
  on Individual Educational
      Plans 127–8
  on oral language
      programme 167–8
  on second language
      learners 168–9

causal models
  of co-occurrences with
    dyslexia 82–3
  of dyslexia 53–9, 70–4
changes in development
  of dyslexia 59–61
Chinn, Steve 196
Clarke, Paula 158, 159
classroom support
  accommodations in 222–4
  ADHD 204–5
  auditory working memory 186–7
  developmental coordination
    disorder 212–13
  dyspraxia 212–13
  listening comprehension 183–4
  oral language 181–5
  organizational skills 188–9
  parental involvement 174–5
  phonic decoding skills 173
  phonological processing
    skills 172–3
  reading comprehension 181–6
  reading speed 174–5
  spelling 176–81
  study skills 188–9
  written narrative skills 187–8
co-occurrences
  and ADHD 90–5, 202–10
  assessment of 135–48
  causal models of 82–3
  and developmental coordination
    disorder (DCD) 95–8, 210–16
  and developmental language
    disorder (DLD) 74–80, 83–4
  and dyscalculia 85–90, 194–201
  and dyspraxia 95–8, 210–16
  identification of 131–5
  support for 193–217
cognitive model of dyslexia
  54, 56–8, 72–3
cognitive predicators 26
complex difficulties 225–34
comprehension monitoring 65–6
computer simulations 29–31
connectionist models
  of reading 30
Connections in Mind 203
Cooper, M. 90
Cunningham, Anne 24

delay aversion 92
Department for Education
  227, 228
Developing Reading Comprehension
  (Clarke) 159
development of dyslexia 74–8
developmental coordination
  disorder (DCD) 95–9,
  134–5, 142–4, 210–16
developmental language disorder
  (DLD) 74–80, 83–4, 117–18
dietary approaches to ADHD 207–8
Dowker, Ann 196
Dubicka, B. 221
Duff, Fiona 152
Dynamo Maths 196
dyscalculia 85–90, 132–3,
  135, 137–9, 194–201
dyslexia
  and ADHD 90–5
  assessments for 117, 123
  behavioural model of
    dyslexia 58–9
  biological model of 54–6, 70–2
  brain difference 55–6, 71
  case studies on 62–3, 78–80,
    89–90, 94–5, 98–9
  causal models of 53–9, 70–4
  changes in development
    of 59–61
  checklist for 105–7
  co-occurrences with 81–100
  cognitive model of dyslexia
    54, 56–8, 72–3
  definition of 52
  development of 74–8
  and developmental coordination
    disorder (DCD) 95–9
  and developmental language
    disorder 76–80, 83–4
  and dyscalculia 85–90
  and dyspraxia 95–9
  existence of 53–4
  multiple deficit model of 74
  neurodiversity model of 52–3
  single deficit model of 70–4
Dyslexia Debate, The (Elliott
  & Grigorenko) 53
*Dyslexia: A Teenager's
  Guide* (Moody) 188

dyslexia teaching
  phonic decoding skills 152–4
  phonological skills 150–2
  reading speed 154–5
  spelling 155–7
  synthetic phonics
    programme 152–4
dyspraxia 95–9, 134–5,
  136–7, 142–4, 210–16

Education, Health and Care
  (EHC) Plan 225–8
Elliott, Julian 53, 54
empowering parents 219–20
examination accommodations
  223–4
executive dysfunction 92

Fast ForWord 164
Frith, J. 57, 221

Gallagher, A. 57
Gathercole, Susan 160, 186
graphemes 155
Grigorenko, Elena 53, 54

Harris, Karen 162
Hatcher, Peter 152
home literacy environment 43–4
homework 189–90
Hulme, Charles 76, 152, 161

identifying co-occurring
  difficulties
  ADHD 133–4
  developmental coordination
    disorder 134–5
  dyscalculia 132–3
  dyspraxia 134–5
identifying literacy difficulties
  assessments for 112–30
  checklist for 105–7
  and Individual Educational
    Plans 103, 111–12
  initial steps after 107–10
  screening for 110–11
Individual Educational Plans
  (IEPs) 103, 111–12, 127–8

IQ tests 113–16
Irlen, Helen 163

Joint Council for Qualifications
  (JCQ) 223

Kelly, K. 173
key words 156, 176–8

later stages of reading
  development 39–41
letter knowledge 32–3
Likierman, Helen 173, 184, 220
listening comprehension 183–4

mappings between sounds
  and letters 31
Martin, J. 221
medication for ADHD 202
Melby-Lervag, M. 161
Moody, Sylvia 188
morphemes 157
Moseley, D. 179
motivating children with
  literacy difficulties 190–1
multiple deficit model
  of dyslexia 74
Muter, V. 46, 61, 173, 184, 220
My Special Alphabet Book
  (Likierman & Muter)
  173, 184, 220

naming speed 39
neurodiversity model of
  dyslexia 52–3
Nicol, C. 179
Nuffield Early Language
  Intervention Screener
  (NELI) 111, 117–18, 184–5
numerosity 86, 194
Numicon 195–6
Nunes, T. 157

oppositional defiant
  disorder (ODD) 91
oral language
  in the classroom 181–5
  difficulties with 65

oral language *cont.*
    expression of 184–5
    in later stages of school 40–1
    parental influence 44
oral language programme
    158–9, 167–8
organizational skills 162, 188–9

Packiam-Alloway, T. 160, 186
parents
    and ADHD 203–4, 205–7
    and dyscalculia 198–9
    empowering 219–20
    and homework 189
    influence on reading
        development 43–5
    reading practice with 174–5
Phillips, S. 173
phonic decoding skills 152–4, 173
phonological awareness
    and alphabetic principle 28–9
    description of 26
    and learning to read 27–8,
        32–3
    measuring 26–7
phonological loop 38
phonological memory 38–9
phonological processing skills
    auditory working memory
        38–9
    in the classroom 172–3
    and dyslexia 150–2
    naming speed 39
    phonological memory 38–9
phoneme representations 58–9
predicator approach 25–6
primitive reflex therapy 164

reading comprehension
    in the classroom 181–6
    difficulties with 64–6, 158–9
    Simple View of Reading
        Comprehension
        model 46–8, 65
    teaching 158–9
    in Year 2 48–50
reading development
    alphabetic principle 32–3, 37–8
    as gateway to learning 23

importance of first two years
    at school 25–6, 37–8
importance of school
    environment 45
later stages of 39–41
letter knowledge 32–3
parental influence on 43–5
phonological awareness
    27–8, 32–3
in Reception Year 33–4
in Year 1 35
in Year 2 35
reading in different
    languages 42–3
reading speed 154–5, 175–6
Reception Year
    reading development in 33–4
repeated reading intervention
    155, 165–6, 169, 175–6, 215
Rucklidge, J.J. 208

screening for literacy
    difficulties 110–11
second language learners 42–3,
    119–20, 144–7, 168–9
SENCos
    in literacy difficulties
        identification 109
SEND tribunal process 226–7
sensory integration therapy 211
Seymour, Philip 43
Simultaneous Oral Spelling
    (SOS) 156, 177–8
Simple View of Reading
    Comprehension
    model 46–8, 65
single deficit model of
    dyslexia 70–4
Snowling, Margaret 39,
    40, 52, 57, 72, 76
Sound Linkage Programme
    152, 165, 172–3
spelling 155–7, 176–81
Stanovich, Keith 24
story-telling skills 182–3
Strong, G. 164
study skills 162, 188–9
synthetic phonics programme
    34, 152–4

Teaching Literacy to Learners with Dyslexia (Kelly & Phillips) 173
technology, use of 220–2
Tickle, Louise 228
tinted lenses 163
Trouble with Maths, The (Chinn) 196

Wechsler, D. 114
Wechsler Intelligence Scale for Children (WISC) 114
What Works Best For Children And Young People With Literacy Difficulties? (Brooks) 173

whole-book reading 154
written narrative skills 162, 187–8

Year 1
    reading development in 35
Year 2
    reading comprehension in 48–50
    reading development in 35